THE HEALING PATH

Part One of Three:

Stay Present

Lisa Chase McFarland

Copyright © 2024 by Lisa Chase McFarland

All rights reserved. No part of this book may be reproduced by any mechanical, photographic, or electronic process, or in the form of a phonographic recording; nor may it be stored in a retrieval system, transmitted, or otherwise copied for public or private use—other than for "fair use" as brief quotations embodied in articles and reviews—without prior written permission of the author.

ISBN: 978-1-965016-03-9

1st edition, September 2024

Contents

Preface 5

Introduction 11

Chapter One:
A Mother's Grief 15

Chapter Two:
Overview of the Healing Path
Part One: Stay Present 43

Chapter Three:
Steppingstone #1: Stillness
An End to Spinning 46

Chapter Four:
Steppingstone #2: Equanimity
The Intentional Act of Welcoming Everything 64

Chapter Five:
Steppingstone #3: Observation What's Here? 91

Chapter Six:
Closing Thoughts 110

Afterword 117

Preface

The Healing Path is a conversation about pain and suffering. Despite the inevitability of death and the guarantee that we will all die, we ignore it. After a few clichés and a funeral, those of us who have experienced profound loss find that we are expected to get on with moving on. ASAP.

The process of trying to "move on" in the aftermath of my losses governed about twenty-five years of my life. But after all this time, I am finally starting to feel like I can participate in my life, and what I have learned is so surprising that I am compelled to share my experience.

I am not promising anything. I don't know for sure that things I have experienced will help you or anyone else. But I do know that suffering in silence nearly suffocated me to the point of my own demise. Dozens, if not hundreds of times. I don't believe I am unique in this way.

I have experienced on a visceral level the isolating and deadening wake that follows a sailed ship and the finality of death. Until we give our pain the dignity and honor it deserves, I believe we will stay silenced and suffocated, floating around looking for a place to dock, to the point of our own undoing, be it swift or death by a thousand cuts.

Grief is complicated. I am not healed, nor am I fixed. My heart is still broken in places that will never mend. But I have found a way to respect my pain, something I didn't know was possible. I've been running, and I'm tired now. I don't want to run anymore. Maybe you are tired of running also.

Until our culture gives itself permission to grieve loss and feel pain, we have to take steps to do this on our own. The path is not for the faint of heart. If you are reading this now, you are probably already in the throes of living multiple identities as I did. There is the *you* who is there when you go to sleep and first wake up, and there is the *you* who shows up during the hours in between.

Regardless of what has happened, if you are still here, you have grit, endurance, and some inclination, even if only a whisper, that there remains the possibility of living your one true identity. Even if you feel complete despair, there is some part of you that wants to stop numbing, suffering, and climbing uphill. There is a thread of our humanity that won't let us give up on ourselves, despite our best efforts to tap out of a life that is excruciatingly painful.

Excruciatingly painful. Having a miscarriage as a new bride, like I did. Or burying your only daughter, like I did. Or holding your tiny son on the day of his birth as he took only short sips of life from his small nose before dying in your arms, like I did. Excruciatingly painful, like my mind, body, and soul were on fire. Excruciatingly painful, like I would do anything to make it stop.

And I did try to make it stop. Everything and anything. Changing careers. Moving. Educating myself. Getting therapy. Meditating. Praying. Numbing. Begging and pleading for solace. And maybe you have tried, too, to ease the suffering from losing a loved one, a home to a fire, a relationship, or a career.

Maybe your project and dream lost its funding. Maybe you are adopted and can't reconcile the pain of having been entrusted to more capable hands. Maybe you woke up one day and your life partner who lay in silence next to you didn't wake up also. Maybe you were wounded in acts of war. Or perhaps an auto accident or senseless act of violence took someone from you or stole your own ability to participate in life the way others seem to be able to.

Perhaps you're living a charmed life, and none of this applies to you. Yet.

However, loss is universal. Pain is inevitable. It's part of the deal when we humans agree to keep breathing. But suffering in silence doesn't have to be part of the deal. Suffering is a choice we can make or not make. And before making choices about something so critical, we first need conversations—about death, dying, change, and impermanence. Once these words lose their stigma, we may be able to pave a way forward.

There is no ready-made healing path. There is only the invitation to build our own path of healing today. In our new *now,* we may be without our loved one, without our legs, without our security, or without a roof over our heads. In our new *now,* we vote for the life we want and still believe is possible, with each action or nonaction. In our new *now,* we move forward, not in spite of our pain but because of it.

I am bruised. I am scarred. But I am also beautiful. Chronic bruising and scarring can suffocate the beauty that lingers beneath the pain if we are not careful. I have found that when I let everything come together with tenderness and take small steps toward self-care, the thick haze of bodily and emotional insults gets incrementally less dense. When that happens, it all feels perfect.

Over the last few years, I have been learning to lean into these "perfect" moments. They are simply blissful. I thought they were impossible for me, but when I stopped compartmentalizing everything I began to see and feel the coming together of things. Even though it's not a place I can stay forever, it's a lot better than living multiple identities and thinking I missed something that everyone else seems to have been gifted.

I don't have answers, but I have these paused, blissful moments that have shown up when I was busy trying to "move on." The kind of moments that stop time. The gap after an exhale that allows a little shimmer of light to transcend it all. I have had these glimpses of acceptance, of "being okay-ness," and in them, I find the most miraculous evidence of divine presence. Just one of those moments, as fleeting as it may be, is compelling enough to inspire me to open to more in hopeful anticipation of feeling such a moment again someday.

If you are grieving, regardless of the circumstances, you may have a lingering suspicion that there has to be some other way to do the excruciatingly painful things, and for whatever reason, you haven't given up on that quest.

Thank God you have not. There are ways to ease our suffering, and we can learn to help ourselves. No matter how horrifically or disastrously bruised and scarred your mind, body, and soul may be, you are also beautiful. There is a tender bliss that awaits you on a path of healing. The emergence of these time-stopping moments can inspire you to continue the longing, even if you haven't gotten your own glimpse of one yet.

Once you get a glimpse into what is possible when you wear your scars as medals, you want to do more of it. In my years of grieving, there have been recurring themes, signs, and invitations. I have organized these into ten principles, one of which or all of which or none of which may resonate.

Each principle has been coupled with a set of actions you can try. Or not. I invite you to investigate with a spirit of curiosity and patience. Try to keep your mind open. When it gets uncomfortable, remind yourself that you have already tried everything else, so you have nothing to lose. A playful, albeit heavy heart may help you through the awkwardness of trying new things.

The contents of this book are divided into four sections. The first will introduce you to my personal experiences with grief as they pertain to motherhood. The remaining sections consist of the first three steppingstones, which will be presented and followed by suggested actions that may help you develop your understanding of each. Most of these actions are free, are available to you around the clock, and don't require anything other than your willingness to experiment.

Building a healing path is not a linear process. In fact, if any of this book's action steps land, you may find developing them to be a lifelong project as I have. The only thing required to get started is to formally admit to yourself that based on outcome, the principles you have been accessing and the tools you have reached for aren't easing the suffering you feel.

The Healing Path, Part One: Stay Present may be digested in small, bite-sized pieces over a long period of time. Or if you have the appetite and the support, you may gobble up the content in large doses over a few days. But pace yourself. Healing is not a sprint—it's more of a marathon—and you will have to agree to unconditionally and lovingly allow yourself to indulge in the process of discovery. Sometimes when we try new things, they don't fit, so we reach for relief. But the relief is short-lived, hardly relief at all. As we learn to practice, this fresh energy can take on delicate momentum of its own.

We are not alone, and I make this commitment: I am right here with you, trying to find my own way. Even as I write these words, I know I have only scratched the surface of what there is to learn about this life. I urge you to commit to yourself, to be kind and gentle, and to remind yourself as much as you may need to that grief is inevitable but that perhaps suffering is not. Let's see.

Introduction

At fifty-four, having grieved more than half of my life, I reflect back on my losses and realize there is substantially more to grief, pain, and suffering than meets the eye. I was introduced to death as a young person, and since being a teenager, I have been challenged with loss on many levels.

Sometimes I think that my life has been a tragic series of funerals. The first I attended was for an elderly neighbor who died while I was in grade school. My second funeral was that of a beloved former teacher who died when I was in junior high. During my sophomore year of high school, I mourned the loss of a friend who had been tragically and violently killed. I was a senior when another friend also died tragically and violently.

Perhaps I was numb from losing those two peers so brutally and didn't yet have the capacity to process the profound shock of it all. Or perhaps I was intentionally trying to stay frozen in an effort to "protect" myself from potential future pain. Either way I don't remember many funerals until the one that came in September 1997.

I vividly remember this burial service—the one I planned when I was twenty-seven for my only baby daughter, Alexis. When I was thirty-two, I most regrettably did not plan a funeral for my infant son, Emmanuel, who died on the day of his birth.

With the death of Emmanuel in 2002 came the cessation of my lifelong dream to carry, deliver, and raise a healthy baby. My own medical condition had become so vulnerable during his birth that I knew I had to stop putting myself in danger. My focus shifted to managing the relentless challenges of raising our son Zach, who was nearly four years old by then.

We were running on life's treadmill, and there were no breaks for grief. There were barely breaks for a shower. I pursued a new career, working as a pediatric ICU nurse, which evolved into a successful legal nurse consulting practice. My husband, Ernest, was busy attending night law school while working full time in Washington, D.C. These pursuits helped us get out of bed in the morning while also distracting us from all the pain that was brewing patiently, quietly, and steadfastly, waiting for us to acknowledge it.

By any standards, a lot was accomplished during that time. My self-improvement projects (from going to nursing school and studying for boards to acting as an RN for my special-needs, feeding-tube-dependent son) were more like distraction contracts. I signed them with ambition and with a secret and maybe unconscious hope that they would keep me from thinking about Alexis dying.

Suffering is not the result of what happens to us. Rather, it's the result of the choices we make when loss inevitably shows up. Some of the choices I made when my children died led to more suffering. They were choices that seemed to dull the pain, whether through distraction, physical and emotional turmoil, or just plain anesthetizing through a plethora of unhealthy habits.

Most of the choices I now make have helped me to pave an alternative path. This path is not a narrow one of numbing, running, and white-knuckling my way through the day. This path is wide open. There is room for everything. The foundation is paved with compassion and love instead of resistance and debilitating fear. I am open-hearted instead of closed and inaccessible. I have learned that there are things I can do to take care of myself and my grief that just weren't possible until I allowed all of me to get to know my pain.

Forging a path of healing is not about getting to a destination. It's not about forgetting where we've been or even about easing the aches, pains, and agony of grief. The healing path is about finding ways to love ourselves—not despite what we've lost but as a direct result of what we've lost.

I wrote this book to share concepts, philosophies, and actions that have enabled me to make better choices while creating my own healing path through grief. I've relinquished the goal of getting "healed" or "past" or "over" my pain. I've stopped running. I now allow my pain—and even welcome it—to exist in the daylight with all the parts of me.

I am rapturous. I am decimated. And I am everything in between. In this book, I share these balms for grief wounds with the sincere hope that one or two will resonate with you and will actually help you forge your own path of reduced suffering. Notice that I didn't say less grief. If we can truly absorb that grief is not the enemy, we may actually have a chance to live full, vibrant, loving, and creative lives. Grief and suffering are not the same thing. Perhaps the next several pages will demonstrate the difference between the two and you will feel empowered to allow your grief while learning to release the suffering.

One

A Mother's Grief

Please allow me to introduce you to my family. Ernest is my best friend, life partner, and husband. He is also the father of our four children: Michael (yes, we named him even though he was tiny), whom I miscarried in September 1994; Alexis Layton, who arrived in August 1996 and died in September 1997; Zachary Alan, who arrived in May 1999 and is still thriving; and Emmanuel, who arrived and died in April 2002.

In the medical world, my reproductive classification is G4, P3, 1L, which means I have carried four pregnancies, resulting in three live births and one living son, Zach, who is nearly twenty-five. Officially, I have lost three babies. Let me tell you a little about them.

Michael

It was a Saturday night in late August 1994. I was wearing a purple pantsuit with a matching blouse I loved to celebrate a friend's bachelorette party for her upcoming October wedding. It was the same outfit I had worn on my honeymoon in Bermuda, just a few months prior.

We were barhopping in Syracuse, New York. Thirty years ago, we had bachelorette "parties," not bachelorette "vacations." The night was considered a success if the bride had a blast and everyone got home safely. We moved from place to place in this college town and finally called it a night in the wee hours of the morning. It was a great success, but come Sunday morning, I had no energy. I felt nauseous and unsteady. *I really must have had too much to drink*, I thought to myself. I felt like crap.

It was an inconvenient time to feel unwell because Ernest and I had to pack up that day and make the three-hour drive back to Buffalo for the start of the work week. I was sluggish and felt sick, but I pressed on despite feeling unable to do so. Our FIDO attitude—short for "Fuck It, Drive On"—was in high gear. FIDO is a military acronym I learned from Ernest when we were teenagers. It basically means, "Nobody cares. Keep it moving." FIDO became our household philosophy, but you'll notice that it's *not* included in the ten stepping stones that pave the healing path. FIDO is more like a deep hole that one foot slips into and can't escape from. FIDO as a life strategy is *not* a plan—but we didn't know that in 1994.

So FIDO, we got back home late Sunday night, and the early Monday morning routine was underway much faster than I would have liked. At work that day, I still didn't feel well, and at some point it occurred to me that I could be pregnant. And in fact I was. I was pregnant with the first of four lives that would come into the universe through Ernest and me.

I was so excited. *Oh! I'm not hungover. I'm pregnant!*

The pregnancy lasted only about a week before the fertilized egg became embedded in one of my fallopian tubes. I went into the hospital for emergency surgery to safely remove both. We later came to know this life as "Michael" and so named him, even though he died in the early stages of the first trimester.

I didn't know it at the time, but this loss of Michael was only the first of several gut-wrenching losses that would become part of our family fabric. I felt terrible and spent the next couple of months depressed and stricken by grief.

But FIDO was our family motto, and that's exactly what we did. We moved on, literally, as we relocated in early 1995 from Buffalo to Washington, D.C., where Ernest completed his work-study program with the federal government and graduated that spring.

New to the area surrounding the nation's capital, I started to look for work as a young entrepreneur. I was thrilled when my doctor told me I needed to wait only ninety days before attempting another conception. By winter 1995, we were well in the clear to regain focus on our goal to have a baby. And we did. A year later, I was pregnant with Alexis.

Alexis

It was December 1995. I felt like shit, and this time I *knew* I was pregnant. But none of the expensive over-the-counter tests were confirming what I felt I knew. Finally one morning, I walked into the bathroom and, for some reason, decided to remove the completed pregnancy test from the garbage bin. I had taken the test the night before and threw it away because it appeared to be negative. But in the morning light and after hours of processing, there it was! A tiny, red, second line in the test window, confirming pregnancy.

I called to Ernest to show him! We were ecstatic, elated, and so excited to share this news with our extended family over the holidays. What could be a better Christmas gift than pregnancy? We traveled to Syracuse, where we would spend those holidays, and despite the warnings to keep pregnancies quiet for the first trimester, we didn't care. We told everyone. And I felt terribly sick from day one.

In January 1996, we vacationed in Jamaica at my then-stepfather Jeff's home at the Tryall Club. I remember the terrible 1996 snowstorm that shut down the federal government and all businesses in Washington, D.C., for roughly a week. Ernest was relieved that he would not have to clock vacation days at work because the government was closed. I was working in the private sector and would have no such luck. But we were content to be in a beautiful climate, missing the debilitating ice storms and traffic accidents back home.

The Tryall Club is a magnificent place and is the most luxurious setting where I have ever vacationed. We were incredibly fortunate that we were there, and we would return many times over the next several years. Everything we could possibly want or need was at our fingertips, and the massive home sat right on the edge of the water and had a completely stunning view of Montego Bay. We were literally "living the dream"!

But I felt terrible. I was nauseous and tired, and most of the time, I felt like I was recovering from a night of heavy college drinking and no sleep. I'd heard all the old wives' tales about morning sickness. Friends and relatives would say, "The sicker you are, the healthier the pregnancy" or "This passes after the first trimester" or "You will feel better soon—it means the pregnancy is really taking hold."

I can't say I was comforted by any of these comments, but I accepted them nonetheless. After all, what did I know? I was to become a first-time mom and would have to learn everything. Little did I realize how far, deep, and wide "everything" would go.

The sickness did not resolve. I felt terrible for the entire pregnancy. I continued working at my job, nibbling on salty snacks, sipping on soda, and getting horizontal any chance I had. At some point, we became aware of some red flags with the pregnancy beyond the excessive nausea: there might be abnormalities with its progression.

Late in the second trimester, I was diagnosed with "IUGR," short for "intrauterine growth restriction," as the fetus was not growing in a manner consistent with norms and expectations. Also, there was an ongoing, documented condition of low amniotic fluid, which was identified via ultrasound.

None of these things meant losing the pregnancy—they just meant losing the excitement and even the "romance" that can come with the inception and expectation of new life. This was no fun. I was scared to death. And I felt like throwing up all day, every day.

As we moved into the hot summer of 1996 and closer to my delivery due date, my physician suggested we prepare for the early arrival of this baby. And at a routine checkup in August, with a gestational age of roughly thirty-seven weeks, I was sent straight from the doctor's office to the hospital for induction of labor. As I understood it, when the external environment becomes safer for the infant than the uterus, delivery is indicated. (Years later, I gained an extensive knowledge of this when I became a registered nurse in the field of pediatric intensive care.)

Labor was induced on Thursday, August 8, and on Saturday, August 10, 1996, Alexis was delivered by Cesarean section, Ernest by our sides. Alexis weighed four pounds, ten ounces. We were parents of a precious, little angel baby girl.

The moments, days, weeks, and months that ensued, concluding in the death of our precious, little angel baby girl a year later in September 1997 linger with the memories that forever haunt me. These memories also remind me of who I am.

Alexis lived thirteen months and five days after her arrival. Ultimately, her body would succumb to its inability to function properly. An "FTT" (aka "failure to thrive") diagnosis began to follow her, as we dove into the unknown abyss of the infant and pediatric medical world, trying to understand why she could not maintain her weight without the help of tubes and catheters.

Multiple diagnoses would follow. By her first birthday in August 1997, we made the treacherous, unthinkable, unimaginable decision to cease the hematological interventions and therapies treating her aplastic anemia.

This decision did not come easily. We had spent months as an "in-patient" family at Children's National Medical Center (CNMC) in Washington, D.C. From bone marrow biopsies to blood draws, MRIs, EKGs, EEGs, and every other test I had ever heard of, results were not revealing a lot of hope for a quality of life that would be worth fighting for. We met with clergy, medical people, social workers, and ethics committees.

We drafted a mission statement, which we literally wrote down and kept on a piece of paper in the hospital room. Every time we had to make one of hundreds of decisions, we referred back to our joint mission, which was to provide a comfortable and thriving life for our daughter—until we couldn't.

I had no idea at the time that this idea of a mission statement could play such an important role in the unfolding of the weeks that followed. I highly recommend this level of clarity and specificity to anyone who has to make an important decision. When the vision is clear, it can easily be tested. Once we could no longer protect her, we had to let her go.

On the night of Monday September 8, 1997, we brought Alexis home from the hospital with the support of hospice and nursing care. At that point in time, she had a central line, a small catheter that accessed a major vein into her heart. Alexis also had a feeding tube. But after her intestines collapsed, the tube was no longer functioning as anything but a drain, much like a colostomy, for her stomach contents.

Alexis was swollen from immunosuppressive therapy and prednisone. She looked exhausted. We knew we were doing the right thing, but that didn't make it easy. Bearing witness to her physical demise was as close to intolerable as I could get.

We spent the next couple of days just literally being in the moment. I remember a hospice nurse visiting on Thursday September 10. She said to me, *So is this just kind of like a vigil, where you are waiting for her to die? Maybe it will be a while before her body gives out."*

First of all, really? As an end-of-life "professional," you were asking me to use literal words and language to communicate what was happening? I didn't know what a vigil was. I didn't know how long Alexis had to live. I only knew I didn't want to share whatever time she had left, with that hospice nurse or anyone else for that matter. If she had a day or a year to live, I was not going to miss one breath.

So yes, I guess it did become kind of a vigil. That weekend, we had family and close friends visiting and allowed Alexis to be held and comforted for the last time by those who loved her.

Between Saturday and Sunday of that weekend, there was food, quiet music, dim lighting, and soft speech. There were candles burning, and there was a calm that held the first floor of our townhouse together. The energy was almost as anticipatory for her passing as it had been for her birth. I found this ironic, and I breathed slowly through those hours. It was such an unchartered experience, to be anticipating death. The fact that I had to learn that experience surrounding the death of my daughter made this all the more a surreal experience for me.

By Sunday September 14, Alexis began bleeding from her gums and g-tube stoma (the opening in her stomach where the gastro tube sat). Her platelets had dropped so low that she would either bleed to death or we would need to get platelets transfused immediately. We did *not* want her to die of profuse bleeding: this had been anticipated and decided before we ever left CNMC on September 8.

So we had a plan, and there was no decision to make. Ernest, Alexis, my mother, and I got into the car and headed for the ER at CNMC, about an hour away. When we got there, we were met by friends who knew what was happening. We were greeted by medical and nursing staff, some of whom were very well known to us by that point. They knew why we were there.

Alexis was not new to transfusions. Once her bone marrow began failing early in summer 1997, her body required infusions of red blood cells, plasma, and platelets. She wasn't producing any of these components on her own. But transfusions seemed to bring hope with them. We were used to seeing Alexis perk up after the lethargy of low counts was ameliorated. The more she needed blood, the less active she would become. But the transfusions seemed to bring a restoration that would comfort all of us. They had done so all summer. But not this time.

After Alexis received her four-hour platelet transfusion in the ER, Ernest, Mom, and I packed her up and got back in the car to head home. She was still pale and lethargic. Mom sat with her in the back seat and would later share that she noticed some of the other ominous symptoms of decline we had been warned about, symptoms that would be followed by the onset of death. Mom didn't tell us at the time, but she knew what was happening.

From Sunday night to Monday night, Alexis never rebounded. The platelets brought the bleeding to a halt but did not impact the inevitability of death as the unavoidable outcome. We held her, rocked her, sang to her, gave her palliative medications, and prayed and prayed for her comfort.

Then in the deafening stillness of that dark September evening, at 10:25 p.m., Alexis lifted her head from over my heart where it had been resting all night and day and opened her eyes for the first time in thirty-six hours. She looked widely into my eyes and drew her last breath. Her head slowly fell back to my chest, and time stopped. It was over. Alexis was gone.

Zachary

I suppose it is natural to start thinking about seeking another pregnancy after a child has died or there has been a miscarriage. Just as we had sought medical input following my ectopic pregnancy in 1994, we tried to learn what we could about what had happened to Alexis and whether future healthy children were possible.

Ernest and I traversed genetic studies both in our own research and in the opening of our family and individual DNA to Children's National Medical Center (CNMC and the National Institutes of Health (NIH. We wanted to be certain that Alexis's illness and death were not something more than the "fluke" that every medical person kept trying to convince us it was. After months of testing, there was nothing conclusive or diagnostic.

At the end of the genetic analysis process, we were told that about one in one hundred live births have some kind of "anomaly"; this can be as benign as an extra freckle or as malignant as aplastic anemia (part of Alexis's cause of death). So we felt we essentially had a free pass to go back to baby-making.

I had started my accelerated nursing school program in September 1998. We had wanted to wait a full year before trying to become pregnant again after losing Alexis in 1997, so as we moved into fall we decided to go for it.

Several weeks later, Ernest and I were playing indoor soccer on a co-ed team we had put together. Games were Sunday evenings, and they were usually followed by a social hour of one kind or another. We would inevitably hang around the soccerplex after games and chat up the other players over a beer. Or we would migrate to someone's house, including our own, to talk shop and ignore the fact that the work week was starting. We were young then, so we could usually pull this off without a problem.

One Sunday night during the game, I was running with the ball, when I suddenly fell, bracing myself with my right arm. I literally heard the bone break as it connected with the turf. I picked up my right arm by using my left hand to cradle it and started to make my way off the field.

We joke about this exchange now, but at the time Ernest, who played coach and goalie, was rushing me off the field. *Fresh legs! We need fresh legs! Get Lisa off the field*! It was surreal to me because adrenaline had kicked in: everything was muffled and in slow motion.

I just kept saying *I heard it,* meaning I "heard" it break. Ernest kept responding, thinking I was saying *I hurt it.* Ernest shouted, *We know you're hurt. Get fresh legs on the field!* I stepped into the players' box and waited it out. After the game, we went to the ER for X-rays.

Any chance you are pregnant, Mrs. McFarland? The ER staff wanted to know if it was safe to take an image.

Nope, I responded confidently. It had only been a few weeks since we had started "trying" to conceive again; there was no way it could have happened that fast. But that Sunday evening in October, just a year following the loss of Alexis, I left the hospital with two diagnoses: a right radial fracture and a positive pregnancy test result.

Since I was in nursing school in Virginia and driving a stick shift car that we shared, things got interesting fast. I couldn't shift the gears with my right hand because it was in a cast. I also couldn't take anything for pain. I started getting schedules for "planes, trains, and automobiles" to get to my classes and clinicals in Virginia while I lived in Maryland.

I would take the Metro in Maryland to a commuter bus in Arlington, Virginia. I would take that bus to the campus, attend twelve-hour days of lectures, labs, and practicals, and then reverse the order of my travels to get home that night. The twelve-hour day turned into sixteen hours with a two-hour "travel time requirement" for the commute, which was normally a forty-five-minute drive.

I was without the use of my right hand, was in pain, and felt like vomiting, just as I had during my pregnancy with Alexis. I was nauseous, dizzy, unable to eat or drink much. I could barely keep up with the treadmill of my life.

Enter the family motto: FIDO. Fuck It, Drive On. We did.
But I took it one day, one course, one commute, one purge session, and one exam at a time. Eventually the wrist pain resolved, and the cast came off. I could now drive. Days were still long because I was still feeling (and getting) sick all the time. Nothing like holding the plastic urinal for adult patients in one hand while reaching for the trash bin with the other so I could mitigate the mess by throwing up in it. But I got through it.

In spring 1999, I was placed on bed rest and was trying to keep food down. I drank Ensure and laid on my left side most of the time as the doctor had instructed. Zach's due date was the end of June, so I was trying my best to finish my courses and clinical for that semester before he arrived. If I could get that done, I would have only one semester of courses left until I could sit for the nursing state board exam.

I had the best fortune of studying with several amazing women who had my back. They would come up to my townhouse for study groups since I needed to stay horizontal (no Zoom options at that point in time). They'd quiz me and talk things through until we all successfully completed that semester. I am forever grateful.

Then, just as I had been when I was pregnant with Alexis, I was sent from a routine doctor visit directly next door to the hospital to be prepared for delivery. When I called my husband to tell him, he thought it was a joke. It wasn't.

An emergency C-section later, on Monday, May 24, 1999, Zach was born. He weighed just under four pounds. He immediately sustained a tear to his right lung, which was not yet developed. A chest tube was placed, and Zach was intubated and put on a breathing machine. From there, he went to the NICU (neonatal intensive care unit), where his life was touch and go for several days.

A couple of days in, the neonatologist came to my room and said that Zach's only chance for survival was to undergo "ECMO" treatment, a process they could not implement at the hospital where we were patients. Zach would need to be transferred to Georgetown Hospital, where his blood would be removed, oxygenated, and returned to his body (similar to the process of dialysis) by machines until his body could do this for itself. ECMO—or extracorporeal membrane oxygenation—sounded daunting.

We were warned about the severity of Zach's condition. We were asked to acknowledge our understanding that his small size gravely decreased his chance of responding to the ECMO treatment and that survival would be unlikely. But we could try, and we quickly decided we would.

Then something miraculous occurred. Before the time came to transfer him to Georgetown, Zach started responding to the ventilator. His need for manual oxygenation (which was provided by human hands and a neonatal Ambu bag) started to decline. He was able to rest on the ventilator for longer and longer periods of time without needing the manual Ambu oxygenation.

Within forty-eight hours, Zach was removed from the ventilator and was sustaining himself on oxygen supplements and a myriad of complex machinery provided in the NICU. He would stay in that same hospital for the next six weeks as we tried to understand his complicated, fragile, and tiny body. We worked around the clock to get him to eat by mouth and gain weight.

When Zach was around six weeks old, we were able to bring him home. Oh, what a moment that was! For a very short period, Zach and I were able to bond, no nurses, no interruptions, no machines (other than the cardiac harness to alert us if his heart rate dropped). It was a precious honeymoon for all three of us, and we thought we were finally out of danger.

We weren't. Just a year after that broken wrist revealed the news that Zach was coming, we were already beginning to understand that his expanding list of diagnoses was serious and complex. His health situation would continue to tug at our heartstrings with every passing moment. Having already buried Alexis just two years prior, it was all we could do not to purchase the empty cemetery plot that sat next to Alexis's burial site in case Zach died.

But there was no time for that. Ernest was researching like crazy, while I was trying to get Zach to eat. Ernest aggregated several if not all of the symptoms that Alexis exhibited and that Zachary's body was also presenting. Added to Zach's diagnosis of "failure to thrive" were his many indicators of ill health: relentless fatty and greasy stools that stained clothes and furniture, projectile vomiting, weight loss, irritability, and low blood counts. All of it haunted us.

I won't forget the day Ernest walked into Children's National Medical Center. It seemed everyone knew us at CNMC, as Alexis and Zach were both treated there. Ernest tossed a stack of papers on the hospital room couch, which also served as my bed.

Please tell me this is not what we are dealing with, Ernest said as he shared with me what his research had uncovered. *This "Shwachman-Diamond" thing, it's genetic.* Ernest would go on to explain that the symptoms were malabsorption, failure to thrive, frequent infection, and orthopedic complications.

I didn't respond. I just picked up the stack and started reading. Ernest, who had a brilliant legal mind but little medical understanding, had solved the riddle that CNMC and NIH could not. He had found this syndrome in the National Organization of Rare Disorders (NORD) database, and we now had something to learn about, talk about, and bring to the medical teams.

Both of us seemed to be carrying the DNA for this autosomal recessive disease. We wanted to know everything we could about it. There was no genetic test for Shwachman-Diamond syndrome (SDS) at the time though it was developed several years later. Until then, a symptomatic diagnosis was made.

We attended an SDS meeting in Ohio to spend time with other affected families and to get a better understanding of the disease we thought had taken our daughter and now could also take Zach. My mother met us in Ohio and stayed with Zach at the hotel while Ernest and I attended the many sessions at the conference. We wanted to go deep and wide regarding the implications of this syndrome.

Most notably, I recall a hematologist from NIH speaking at that conference. Ernest raised his hand and asked an ambitious question.

We believe our daughter had SDS—she died of aplastic anemia—and we thought our son would also be critically ill and possibly die very young. But he's two and a half years old now, and with support he seems to be holding his own. Is it possible he could live much longer than she did?

Without missing a beat, the physician responded with a statement that still echoes in our audible memory. *It is probably the case that the other shoe hasn't dropped yet for your son*, she said. *SDS does not lend itself to long life spans,* she concluded. She moved to the next audience question.

But her words were already burned into our ears and hearts: *The other shoe hasn't dropped yet.*

As much as we had worked tirelessly for two and a half years trying to stabilize Zach's condition while trying to forget the terror that may await us if Zach's body behaved the way Alexis's did, our bubble was burst wide open. Instead of being empowered, educated, connected, and focused leaving this conference, I felt petrified, deflated, and helpless. Seriously? So our fate is another pediatric funeral? I remember the haze of deep fear that now hung over us as we returned to Maryland. I thought we would feel better after going to the conference, and now I felt so much worse.

One thing we did learn at the conference was that the best chance for survival among SDS patients is a successful bone marrow transplant. I still longed for a healthy child and believed it was possible. Now that we had our pseudo diagnosis of Shwachman-Diamond syndrome, I did some back-of-the-napkin math. It revealed the following.

In a given pregnancy, I would have a:
- 25 percent chance of having a healthy baby who was not sick and who did not carry the SDS gene
- 50 percent chance of having a healthy baby who carried a recessive gene, like Ernest and I do
- 25 percent chance of having a sick baby who not only carried the gene but exhibited symptoms

In my naive and innocent determination to let new life come through my own, I managed to see this as good news. At that point, we'd had three pregnancies and two children, all falling into that last category of affected and symptomatic. The way I saw it, we had a 75 percent chance of having a healthy baby, and since we had already conceived what appeared to be three affected babies, I felt we were "due" a healthy one. Entitlement is a bitch.

With this new statistic in mind (a three-out-of-four chance of having a healthy, unaffected baby) combined with the understanding that Zach's best chance for a bone marrow donor match would be a blood sibling, I had all the data I needed to fire up the baby-making bus again.

Emmanuel

In November 2001, I had yet a fourth positive pregnancy test. We considered that exciting and hopeful news. I was sick again, right away. I was working nights in the pediatric ICU at the local hospital, where I had completed an apprenticeship after passing my state board exam.

One day at a time, sometimes one minute at a time, I was able to navigate the demands of all these situations. This pregnancy had to be our healthy baby, I was sure of it. So I stayed positive and kept putting one foot in front of the other, including juggling all of Zach's care as it became more and more apparent how vulnerable his tiny body was.

Ernest was working days and attending law school in the evenings. I was working full-time nights at the hospital and leading the charge on demanding the best possible care for Zach, who was now 100 percent gastro-tube-dependent and immune-compromised due to his fluctuating blood counts, secondary to SDS.

In retrospect, I imagine people must have wanted to look me in the eye and say, *You're crazy. Why are you doing this again? It's so risky. How will you manage? Aren't you scared? Haven't you been through enough?*

Years later when catching up with one of my lifelong girlfriends, who hadn't known about this fourth pregnancy until after we had already lost Emmanuel, said, *You've got balls, I'll give you that.*

Truth is I didn't feel ballsy, just committed. My sole, and soul, identity since I could remember was simply this: "Mom." That's how I saw myself. I was clear on what my future would look like. I knew I would *do* things in addition to being a mom, but when it came to identity, I felt destined to raise a family. Experiences like this one from my youth resonated so strongly that I felt like I'd already seen my future.

When I had been nearing my twentieth birthday, we were visiting a friend who had four siblings. They lived in a most beautiful and serene home on a lake outside of Syracuse. They were all beautiful people and relentlessly smart. Nearly all five children would earn graduate degrees and become doctors or lawyers.

As Ernest and I sat and chatted with our friend's parents, there was lots going on. Other siblings were coming and going, some with their own friends at the house, creating a joyful chaos. I noticed how graceful and content my friend's mother seemed.

As the house doors open and closed, with kids ranging in age from high school through college coming and going, this woman seemed exactly where she was meant to be. She was glamorous and engaging, and I saw myself in her. The love of that family was palpable. And even though they would have to face their own tragedies as life went on, I had this vision of where I wanted to be: in a beautiful home, with four or five adult children, all of their friends coming and going, and me, sipping red wine, taking it all in. This was the life I wanted. This is the life that beckoned to me.

So yes, I guess that getting pregnant a fourth time was "ballsy," but to me it was just the obvious right choice. Our friends were producing healthy babies all around us. No feeding tubes. No miscarriages. No "failure to thrive" diagnoses to maneuver. I thoroughly believed I was where I was supposed to be—fairly fearless and feeling "on purpose" with another life growing inside me.

I can't say I wasn't warned. When I told Zach's GI doctor, who was also chair of the Department of Gastroenterology at CNMC, about my "back-of-the-napkin math" calculations, he cautioned me.

You know, Mrs. McFarland, those stats reset every time a new pregnancy is conceived. While you think you are due for a "good" result, your body has no idea that you have already had three sick children.

Hmm. I wasn't trying to hear that. I felt entitled, determined, and in resonance with this dream, so I pressed forward with zero regard for reality. FIDO.

When I told my bereavement therapist of my intentions, she, too, cautioned me.

You know, Lisa, you have been through a lot. If this doesn't end up the way you want it to, things could get even harder for you.

I just didn't heed the warnings. I told my therapist that I was longing for a healthy child and that this was the right thing for me. She accepted my proclamation and subsequently helped me focus on opening my heart and mind to whatever may happen with the conception of another life.

I felt invincible and in alignment with my calling to mother more children. I didn't think I could hurt more than I did. I was wrong.

Somewhere around mid-gestation, at the point when sonograms start really looking at the fetus, I got the first round of bad news. Ernest was traveling for work when I visited the perinatologist who was monitoring what was considered to be a high-risk pregnancy. She entered the room with a familiar look—the kind I'd seen from many medical professionals when they had to deliver devastating news but didn't want me to lose my shit in the process. I imagine the last thing this physician wanted to do was what she had to. But she did it.

Mrs. McFarland. this fetus is unwell. There are many indications that the internal organs are not developing in a functional way.

There is a high degree of predictability that this fetus will not make it to term, and if term is reached, there will be multiple complications for the future life of your baby, if able to survive. It is not just a risky gestation for both you and baby: it is pretty much a guarantee that it will be a risky life, perhaps one filled with pain and suffering for your unborn child.

I sat on the exam table, fully clothed and holding the sonogram images that had been handed to me by the equipment technician before the doctor came in and broke my heart. Surely the MD had her conclusions wrong.

I pleaded with her.

But doctor, look at this picture. I can see the heart pumping and feel the movement of this baby. What is it you are seeing? How can you be sure?

In the next thirty seconds, I got the second round of unthinkable news, and my life took a devastating turn. The doctor shared the sonogram image on a larger screen. She showed me how bright some of the areas were and many other things that were alerts for grave concern. The echogenic images told the story. She attempted to hand me a supportive pamphlet, titled something like *Making Decisions for Your Unborn Baby*.

Fuck. This was the only word I could hear in my brain. It was coming from my deflated, if not paralyzed, mother's heart. I knew it was true but didn't want to know.

In that one suspended half minute where I could see the truth of her words in a literal, visual image, reality landed. Tears started flowing, and I politely handed the pamphlet back. *No thank you. I can't do this. I am leaving.*

I quietly picked up my things and headed for the door. The doctor said that I should talk with my husband and that both of us could come back to discuss these findings and our "options."

Because Ernest was traveling for business, we had to talk about this over the phone. I don't have a clear recollection of our conversation. I don't recall whether I told him what the doctor had said, where I was when we spoke, what day it was. These are details that would usually stay with me forever, but this time things were blurry.

My memory basically goes from that day in the doctor's office, with the tech first handing me sonogram pictures and then the doctor handing me a pamphlet, then fast forward to Ernest and me going back to meet with the physician together. This meeting is also blurry. But however it took shape, it was a formal acknowledgment that we would move forward with an induction of labor and that I would be on their schedule early that upcoming Monday morning.

I don't remember what day of the week we heard this news. I don't recall if or how we shared the news with our families. I don't recall talking about it between the two of us. We were mentally back at CNMC in 1997 with the Ethics Committee making end-of-life decisions for Alexis. We knew our roles well. We knew what was coming. We didn't fight it.

Schedules were cleared, appointments were made, labs were drawn, extra help with Zach was put in place, and it would be a couple of days before labor induction Monday morning. That's all I really remember.

Our new and awesome neighbors were scheduled to be married that Saturday evening. Instead of calling in "pregnant," I made a choice that continues to haunt me. I didn't choose to protect myself. I chose to save face, as I always had. Chin up, maternity dress pressed, I attended that wedding with Ernest as if all was well. I don't remember much of the wedding or that evening.

I am haunted that I didn't choose "me," that I chose to keep the peace and go with the flow rather than protecting myself. I can't take it back. But it still hurts.

I suppose I spent that Sunday getting ready for Monday's admission though I don't recall what I did to prepare. Monday morning came soon enough, and there was really nothing else to do or say. If I had to describe the feeling, it is what I imagine soldiers might experience just before initiating an attack or seeing the enemy charge at them and knowing how it would end. We played our roles well. We surrendered.

It was a horror to go through what happened next: medical complications ensued, and Emmanuel would not be born until the following Saturday, six days into induction. Those six days may be described in a future composition, but for now, I will say it was sheer agony. And it ended exactly the way we knew it would—in the death of our son Emmanuel.

My Grief Journey

So yes, I have been pregnant four times, delivered three live babies, and have one living child. Just like my medical chart says: G4, P3, 1L. I think of myself now as a woman who has lost two children and has one living child. Now that you have been introduced to my family, we can talk about grief and its extensive impact on shaping my life.

I don't consider it a badge of honor to be "qualified" to write a book like this. Quite the opposite. If I could go back to my "beginner's mind" (a Buddhist phrase reflecting our open minds at the time of birth), I would be tempted to do it. But instead, I share these experiences, and these words, so that others can suffer less. Not grieve less. But suffer less. Perhaps fewer people will stick to the FIDO motto, which I unsuccessfully utilized, and will instead actually make a soft, safe place for their pain.

When my heart was broken and I was grieving, I looked around in the world for proof that I could survive. I didn't find much in the way of inspiration. I didn't find much in the way of anything. I often say that it's about as popular to talk about grief as it is to talk about aging. No one wants to do it. No one does it.

In my search for some evidence that this was survivable, I found a deadly silence, which further compounded my grief and thus my suffering. I am grateful to the brave and loving authors who had scratched the surface with different publications. I was lucky to have even a few different books that talked about burying our children.

But having respectfully said that, my experience is that our overall culture jumps right into this concept that a prior sense of pre-tragic life is retrievable. *Time heals all wounds*, they tell us. There are gifts of time when it comes to grief, but they don't include healing all wounds. The grief experience is treated like a game that has a start time and will have an end time. But there is no end time. Ever.

And that is the myth that I hope to get us all curious about by sharing my story. How differently would we all respond to loss if instead of treating it like a bump in the road, we invited it to ride in the car with us? I am not saying we have to love it. I am saying that whether we do or we don't love it does not change the fact that the loss is real, ongoing, and omnipresent. The loss does not care whether we love it or not. To make matters worse, there is likely more loss in our future. Death doesn't stop because our hearts don't feel like they're beating anymore.

In the coming pages, I share the first three philosophies—three stepping stones on the path to living with and healing grief—that make up the remainder of *The Healing Path, Part One: Stay Present*. These are ways of being, thinking, and doing that have been an integral part of constructing my healing path. These are not to be completed one after the other, and then we're done. They are more like an array of tools that we can reach for when we stop handling our grief and it starts handling us. Also known as suffering.

Like grief, healing is not an end game. It's a choice, something we act in service of. Not by distracting ourselves, pitying ourselves, or blaming and shaming ourselves. But by making space for and being open to what is here now, without judgment and without that inner critic telling us we should be "better" by now.

My personal calling now is to transcend grief through compassionate presence by helping others do the same. My mission isn't to end grief. Not to numb it. Not to block it, deny it, or resent it. But to transcend it with a welcoming respect and acceptance, by assigning honor and love to these scars, by wearing these scars as medals instead.

Two

Overview of The Healing Path, Part One: Stay Present

The foundation of staying present is pursued and practiced by implementing the first three steppingstones of building this path.

Steppingstone #1: Stillness

This is the practice to somehow summon the courage and the energy to do the hardest, most vulnerable thing you have done since your loved one died: stop moving and become still. This goal to settle in and sit without moving must be done first, before the other steps. This is because cultivating a stillness practice lays the foundation for everything else we will do to build our way to a more balanced and harmonious life.

While it may be tempting to avoid this first step, please do not. Believe me, if there were a possibility to cultivate healing and get relief from pain without sitting still, I would have found it by now! True, a path can be paved without a stillness practice—and maybe you have already ineffectively tried that, as I did for two decades—but the foundation will be shaky.

And we're not going for shaky: we're going for solid. Stillness is the strong foundation where both our pain and our healing can emerge. Stillness points us in the direction of their origins. If we skip this step, all the others will lose their full capabilities. This would be unfortunate because each step in this book holds untapped healing potential.

Steppingstone #2: Equanimity

E-qua-*what*? This concept was new to me also when I was first introduced to it. When it comes to healing, equanimity means just this: learning how to live without bracing against our pain. Sure, it's a foreign word because all we have been taught until now is that pain is bad, so we should run like hell from it. But we can retrain our minds to stop labeling everything as good or bad and instead just allow things to be as they are. When we do this successfully, we find we are more at ease, have more energy, enjoy better health, and are more open to life overall.

This may sound overwhelming, and you may be asking yourself: *Why do I now have to learn something new? I am already burned-out and exhausted just trying to get through each day.*

You would be justified in asking such a question. The answer is that we develop our skill at being "equanimous" because it becomes addition by subtraction. When we hone the skill of resisting the brain's incessant habit of judging our perceived reality, we free up space to be present. We may feel we are giving something up (like perceived control), but in reality, we are gaining personal freedom. Unlike the first steppingstone, this one can be woven in and out of your practice without regard for timing. It is more like a North Star to aim for consistently, less of a box to check.

Steppingstone #3: Observation

It is impossible to see what's here if we are too scared to let our full selves show up. Once we achieve stillness and learn to say yes to everything with equanimity, we move to the third step and get a genuine look at our surroundings and our feelings, maybe for the first time in years! Yes, it is intimidating, but unimaginable benefits may be revealed in the third steppingstone of observation.

If you haven't ever just allowed your whole self to exist, you may be delighted by what you notice (you may also be petrified). But this time—maybe for the first time—you will start to learn to be more of an audience member than the main character. Observation provides an opening for us to see things from different angles; this, in turn, helps us better understand ourselves and others. The focus moves off ourselves as the camera backs out of the close-up shot. That's when the full landscape comes into view.

But first we must end our perpetual movement and get still. As I often say to Zach after trying everything else to get him to do the thing he needs to do, *Now is good.*

Three

Steppingstone #1: Stillness
An End to Spinning

<u>Merriam-Webster definition</u>
Still: "*To become motionless or silent*"

<u>Healing Path definition</u>
Still: "*To become motionless or silent in the face of profound pain, confusion, and chaos such that we allow our grief to authentically arise, flow, and subside regularly*"

Remember the children's game called "statue"? It may not be so popular today, but when I was little, we would run around in the backyard until someone yelled *Freeze!* The first person to move was the loser. It was hard in the heat of summer to stay still after being in full running mode. It was humid, there were bugs, and my heart would beat out of my chest as I concentrated on maintaining my statue pose. The contrast of going from full gallop to full stop made it hard to breathe and difficult to stay still.

It has been decades since I played statue. Other than when it was part of a childhood game, I don't recall "freezing" or "getting still" ever being a virtuous goal. The only times I was still for many years is when I was sleeping, sick, or watching TV. Otherwise, there was no value in not moving. In fact, our busy culture discourages stillness. "Don't let the grass grow under your feet" and other cliché sayings remind us that keeping it moving is a much more worthy target.

Enter profound grief. After our daughter, Alexis, died in 1997, I started learning about meditation. I was reading all types of religious books. Raised Episcopalian, I first turned to the church but discovered that I felt abandoned by God. I then found myself drawn to Buddhism. I learned about the transient nature of all things. This concept resonated.

But meditation did not. I tried it. I didn't get it. So I didn't do it. Instead, I spent the better part of the next twenty years keeping things moving and went on about the business of trying to prove that I could survive my losses. I went to nursing school so I could serve other families, the way ours had been served by nursing professionals. We moved, had more children, sought more education, and stayed in perpetual motion.

About fifteen years after Alexis died, we were living in a beautiful country home that abutted the woods. The natural peace and beauty there felt like home. It was one floor, and our specially abled son, Zach, could navigate all of the space (unlike the former townhouse we had owned). His chronically compromised health was improving significantly.

I had traded in my consulting business for a corporate sales leadership role in the legal industry. I was living in a peaceful space, working in a dynamic career, helping Zach navigate the world, and enjoying more of life than I ever had as an adult. We were surrounded by friends, nature, and good times. It seemed like a dream come true: for the first time, I felt at home in my own skin. I am so grateful to have had that time to remind me that this state of grace was possible.

As goes the Buddhist tradition, all things are transient. After a few years of living what felt like a lottery-winning life (despite the day-to-day challenges of Zach's health and care, I started getting mental nudges. For example, we'd spend an evening with our pals and have a blast. But the next morning, my first thought would be *Lisa, you are wasting time.*

Ew. What? But I was having fun! So I pretended not to hear that message and kept on with my habits, lifestyle, and work. I was getting promoted, learning new technology, and managing Zach's care and medical teams. Some of the health challenges I had suffered in my own body (like chronic back injuries from lifting Zach and his wheelchair to repeated, disabling migraines after suffering a grand mal seizure at a Starbucks seemed to be fading. My body seemed more a friend than an enemy, and I was enjoying feeling healthy for a change.

But the mental nudges continued. They got louder.

Lisa, this is not all you are here for. There is work to be done.

Lisa, you don't fit here.

Lisa, wake up.

These insights went from being casual morning thoughts to messages that jolted me out of my sleep in the night. Over the course of a few years, they were coming more frequently and with more conviction. *Lisa, just because you are good at your day job doesn't mean you should be there.* Huh? I told myself I was getting promoted and earning more money than ever before: I was "in the game" and "playing well."

At some point, I stopped arguing with the nudges and just started listening.

Initially, I had reacted with irritation. *Ugh, I can't be awake at three o'clock. My alarm is going off in two hours. I need rest. I don't want to hear these messages. Can't I just go back to sleep?*

Over time, my response shifted. *Ok, you have my attention. What is it? What are you trying to tell me while I am still and quiet?* I was moving from resistance to curiosity.

That paradigm shift marked the beginning of a season I didn't see coming. Everything changed. My family life, my home, my job, even the way I took care of myself (and the fact that I now *do* take care of myself). The five years that followed would reflect greater and lesser degrees of listening to that nudging voice and getting curious about what it was trying to say.

I was a long way from playing the childhood game of statue, but I did slow down and try to "freeze" at times. I started practicing micro moments of stillness. I had tried implementing a meditation practice for many years, but it wasn't until I read James Clear's *Atomic Habits* and successfully applied his road map for installing a new habit that I attained my goal of establishing a "stillness" practice. I started with such short increments—like meditating for one minute every morning—

that I couldn't "fail." This allowed me to begin showing up regularly, moment by moment, minute by minute, with an increase in tolerance for sitting still.

You may find that the terms "meditation" and "stillness" are often used somewhat interchangeably. This may reflect a misunderstanding about what meditation is and what it is not. That is not the focus of this chapter. Rather, the focus is on inviting you to open to the bigger picture: unless you make space in your life for quiet, whether you call it meditating or getting still or daydreaming, you will not wake up to the fullness of what is here and who you actually are.

Consider a snow globe, the heavy round glass ball holding a winter scene. When the globe is shaken, the floating snowflakes make the entire scene blurry. The scene is still there—the people, the objects, the environment. But it is cloudy when the snow blizzard is in full effect.

At some point, when the shaken snow globe is returned to a shelf or table and left untouched, the snow settles. The flakes rest quietly at the bottom of the foundation, and the scene, the people, and the objects become crystal clear. There is nothing to "do" or "change" or "fix"; rather, the goal is to see that the scene is simply there as it is.

This settling is what is meant when I refer to "stillness." We don't have to be monks in Tibet or live in an ashram to find stillness. It is always here. It is always free. It is always infinite. It is always waiting for us.

The Courage to Seek Stillness

Sitting still is one of the most courageous acts we will ever choose to engage in. It can be sheer terror to remove all distractions and let the snowflakes rest quietly. Stillness is therefore a practice, not an endgame. As with all practices, we develop our skills as we invest our time and commitment again, and again, and again.

There is no "good" time to be still. When life is fantastic, when we are pivoting from one event to the next, maybe advancing in our careers, when we are helping our kids grow and thrive, when we are letting the good times roll, we don't want to be still. Who would want to seek stillness when things are going great? We are too busy in the "going greatness" to seek anything other than that.

Alternatively, when "life" hits the fan—someone is sick, a job is lost, or there is a death or a fire—we resist stillness with even stronger fervor. Why would we want the proverbial snowflakes to settle? What one good reason would there be to take off our armor to show up for what may the most excruciating sixty seconds of our lives? Why not just keep the blizzard going so we don't have to feel the pain?

Another way to think about stillness comes from a lesson I learned from Brené Brown's *The Power of Vulnerability*, in which she writes openly about her own spiritual awakening. She describes an interaction with her therapist. Brown says to her therapist, *I am like a turtle with no shell in a briar patch. I can't be a turtle without a shell in a briar patch. I need a shell. What kind of shell—get some meds—what do you have for me? Give me a shell. Give me like a therapist-sanctified-you-know-whatever shell. Give me a shell!* Her therapist replies, *Well . . . I've got an idea. Why don't you get out of the briar patch?!*

Hearing Brown describe this anecdote in her audiobook rocked me to my core. I had never considered getting out of the briar patch, only surviving it. I had relied on my own various versions of turtle-shell protection mechanisms and observed plenty of them in others. These shells come in endless forms such as food, booze, gambling, social media, perfectionism, hoarding, OCD, constant self-improvement projects, binge TV, excessive drama, relentless "busying" activity, planning for the future, hanging out in the past, and overall *noise*.

But underneath all that noise, there is always the stillness. Getting out of the briar patch means moving out of places that require noise for us to survive and settling instead into a place where we can allow everything to be as it is. I started thinking about what the briar patch was for my life and considering what, if any, power I had to stop seeking shells. Could I find (or create a comfortable and safe place where I could show up as myself, a place where I wouldn't need shells?

There are endless ways to make the case that seeking stillness is a "good" idea. But in my experience (and this was a major shift in my thinking, the reason I choose stillness, day after day, is that it has been the only path home, the only path to myself. Until I learned to allow space to infiltrate the rigid and well-indoctrinated patterns of my brain and behavior, I didn't even realize I was in a briar patch or in a shaken-up snow globe.

This first paver of establishing a time to routinely and consciously stop moving creates a foundation that we learn to land on and trust. We recognize when we're there and recognize when we're not. It is home. And the only way to get to know this place and ourselves is to spend time being still.

Recently when I spent the night at a friend's house, I was about to begin my morning ritual of sitting still. She was taking out her dog and suggested that soon it would be quiet so she wouldn't interrupt my meditation. *Make as much noise as you want!* I replied. *The point of sitting still is to allow everything to be as it is and to resist the tendency to want anything to be different than it actually is.*

This is the essence of the stillness practice. When we strengthen our ability to sit still when there is no crisis, we strengthen our ability to maintain our foundation when turmoil inevitably shows up. And it always shows up.

The title of a Ryan Holiday book says it all: *Stillness Is the Key.* My experience is that stillness *is* the key. It opens the door of possibility. We have no idea what is beyond that door, but the only way to get a mere glimpse is to stop the noise, let the snowflakes settle, take off the protective shells, and play statue whenever we get a minute or two to intentionally put that key in the door and push it open.

Practical Application: Meditation

If you are new to meditation, welcome! And awesome! What if (like me) you have tried meditation many times in the past and have developed bad habits or misconceptions? There are endless resources and DIY meditation guides available to help you learn about the different forms of meditation. There are also helpful apps like Calm and Headspace; many are reasonably priced and are packed with helpful information, structure, and guidance. Additionally, online meditation resources are endless, and many of them offer remote participation.

I suggest that you consider practicing any meditation technique that resonates with you. The technique is unimportant. (See why I love meditation? It doesn't matter how I do it! Simply committing to sit still on a daily basis is the key. No need to wonder if you're doing it "right." Just choosing to be present by sitting still for the duration of time you have committed to means you are already doing it right!

That said, I found that I needed some help along the way, and you may also. The following actions are the steps I took when instituting my own daily meditation practice. It's not complicated, but it ain't easy.

1. *Identify the time of day you will meditate.*
   What part of the day is most consistently available to you? Many people find that morning is an especially effective time of day to meditate. In addition to having control over a morning schedule, the mind is also clearest when we first awaken.

2. *Designate the location where you will meditate.*
   This can be anywhere you feel at home, but it should be consistent. Personally, I have had to extend my own

practice to include meditating in bed, in hotel bathrooms, bedroom closets, and all sorts of creative one-off spaces while I am traveling. With an established practice, that is perfectly reasonable. But when first starting out, we want to decrease the variability of our experience as much as possible. This means returning to the same designated space again and again whenever possible.

Only a small area is needed. You will need enough room to sit cross-legged or with extended legs based on your own body's needs. A particular chair can be a great space as long as you don't tend to fall asleep in it. When community space is limited, closets can be very useful! Bathrooms work as do wide open spaces. The critical element is that when you are in that space, you feel relative peace and harmony and your intention is to strengthen that experience while there.

3. *Personalize the space.*
   You can do this as little, or as extensively, as feels genuine to you. I've seen everything from a pillow in a closet corner to elaborate spaces that are quite large and decorated. The important action here is to make the space uniquely yours for the purpose of establishing your stillness practice.

   There are countless ways to do this, like placing fresh flowers, photographs, and pieces of material, blankets, or clothing that connect you to someone or something calming in the area. Candles (LED candles work safely) and incense can be useful if there is a particular scent that is peaceful for you, such as lavender or vanilla. You can also add personal reading material like holy texts, quotes, and books that inspire you. Maybe someone wrote you a special card that you kept. Having it there would be a nice way to make your space feel welcoming. You may also want a specific cushion or mat that you can designate as your space. If possible, being near some natural light is preferable; this will connect you to nature. A plant or flower or piece of fresh fruit can do that also.

My regular meditation space contains items like a poem I wrote in fourth grade, photographs of my babies, tons of LED candles and live orchids, and letters written to me by loved ones over the years. I also have a diffuser that helps to set a peaceful and pleasant tone. But these are just ideas. What matters most is feeling that the area is uniquely and personally yours.

Settling into the space may not feel familiar at first because it isn't, but it should feel inviting and personal. It's a geography that becomes yours as you carve it out and claim it for yourself again and again.

This is where you will sit in dignity. This is where you will create. This is where you will listen and hear. This is where you will get to know your mind. This is where you will get to know your heart. This is where you will forgive. This is where you will heal. This is where you will love. This is where your idiosyncratic stillness journey will come alive. This place should be held with the highest regard.

4. *Choose the duration of time you will meditate.*

   I highly recommend what finally worked for me: to commit to one full minute for two consecutive weeks at the same time of day (five o'clock in the morning for me). From there, I increased the time to one and a half minutes, then to two minutes, and so on. The driving force behind installing this habit with such a short duration is to make it so easy you can't fail. You designate a ridiculously short time period for the new activity. But you also commit to doing it daily at the same time.

Of course, you can start your stillness practice with more ambition than that—ten minutes every morning or an hour every evening. But if you are new to this courageous practice of showing up for yourself, as yourself, you may find a shorter duration more doable and a bit less intimidating.

Last, with regard to time, be kind to yourself and purchase an egg timer. This is critical to installing the new practice. Without an independent timer, we get distracted by the concept of time. We think and doubt ourselves by creating a narrative to address the insecurity of stopping "on time." This can show up as getting bombarded with mental interruptions: *Am I done yet? Did I do it? Was that it? Did I remember to set the timer? Has it been a minute yet?* And so on. Unless you are ultra disciplined, I don't recommend using your phone or tablet as a timing device as you will risk getting pulled away from your practice before, during, and after.

5. *Establish a dignified posture.*
   Just like your meditation technique, the meditation posture you choose should fit your body. If sitting cross-legged is painful, don't do it. If a pillow under the knees or behind the back is needed, place it there. You may need to experiment with different ways to sit in order to see what is best for you personally. You may need a chair with a straight back or a footstool to keep your knees bent at your hips and not pull on your lower back.

   The essential component here is that you sit upright (or lie down if that is all you are able to do) with your shoulders back and your chin up, facing forward and looking slightly upward. We create our own sitting posture according to our individual body's needs, abilities, and limitations.

   But once there, we sit (or lie) in a way that says, *This is the most important minute of my life.* When you start to slouch or your chin drops, use those moments of noticing to resettle and return to the current moment. Noticing these things are not indicators that you are doing it wrong. Slouching and straightening, inhaling and exhaling, daydreaming and realizing it, and drifting off and coming back are all invitations to be here now. Do not label such moments as bad or unwanted. They are part of the process of getting to know our minds. If we criticize ourselves while we are trying to be still, we can unintentionally build a barricade between ourselves and the present moment.

6. *"Stack" your stillness practice onto a current habit.*
Whether or not we notice, our schedules are made up of the same similar actions repeated again and again. All through the day, we go places and do things that are just part of our routines. We don't think about these actions: they are reflexive.

A powerful strategy when trying to start any new habit is to attach the desired new action to something you already do daily. For example, when establishing my own meditation practice, I habit-stacked it onto brushing my teeth. Once brushing my teeth in the early morning, I was already on my feet and awake. I could easily add the new action of sitting still to that already-part-of-my-routine behavior.

Habit-stacking is certainly not required to establish your new habit, but it can give you an increased likelihood of sticking with the behavior you seek to adopt. And truly, if we are trying to install a new habit and don't have at least one minute a day to commit to practicing, we may need to take a closer look at the habit we tell ourselves we want to install.

7. *Choose your start date.*
Completely up to you! But don't wait! Don't procrastinate! It's too good not to get started!

8. *Commit with indomitable will.*
This is where we must call on our innate understanding of what it means to be an adult. When making this choice,

you are choosing yourself. If you are human, this may be a new concept and an uphill climb. But know this: what you have tried until now has not helped you access whatever type of experience you continue to seek such as peace or nonattachment. This is the perfect chance to practice acting on your own behalf, for your own good, and exponentially for the good of all. Take it seriously.

Meditation is free, flexible, and always available. As humans, we have a nasty habit of thinking we need to "feel" like doing something before we can engage physically. I am suggesting that you take the opposite approach and do it anyway, on the date and time you engineered in your memorialized commitment (see Step 9) and on days when you don't "feel" like it.

Choosing stillness is a personal agreement we willingly make with ourselves. If we identify with a spiritual or religious practice, we may also include that element in our commitment. Such a written statement might include religious language. For example, if God is important to you, you could write, *I will sit still for one minute every morning for two weeks. Deo volente. God willing.*

Beyond your religious and/or spiritual traditions, I encourage you to pause here, right now, for a moment. I invite you to see if you can absorb the idea that this is a uniquely personal journey. You will need this concept to land; otherwise, you risk quitting for a million possible reasons. This is *your* practice. There is no need to imitate anyone else as you bravely try something new. There is no need to grade yourself. There is no need to judge, period.

And there isn't even a need to share what you are doing with anyone, unless you believe doing so will strengthen your ability to practice. That may mean sharing it with no one. It may mean telling your partner or a friend. But use caution. Sharing your intentions with people who are likely to be critical may create an obstacle to the development of your practice. As a reminder, this is a great opportunity to take a first crack at prioritizing your own needs. Go for it!

Returning to the adulthood conversation, committing to a stillness practice means making a decision and sticking to it. Full stop. According to *Merriam-Webster,* the origin of the word "decide" is the Latin word "decidere," which is a combination of two words: "de" means "off," and "caedere" means "cut." When we "decide" to do something, we literally cut off all other possible outcomes except for the one we have committed to.

Taking a voyage into the installation of a new habit like meditation is a worthy but challenging target. I have found this to be especially true if you are not used to engaging in self-care habits (that may be all of us!). Generously give yourself permission to cut off the option of skipping, missing, showing up late, or dropping the ball. No excuses. No rationalizations. No whining. Your commitment is neither good nor bad. It is something you have decided to do. So do it.

Here is a helpful mantra to repeat when you sincerely "don't feel like it" (we all have those days, and it may be most days at first): *It's okay to suck, but it's not okay to skip.* Get yourself to that mat, chair, cushion, altar, path, journal, or wherever it is you need to be to complete the behavior you have committed to. It doesn't have to be your best effort. Just get yourself there.

Do it daily. Don't miss it. And if you have to miss once (it happens!), don't ever miss twice, or you may find yourself back at square one. Own your commitment. Show up for yourself as yourself. Be fiercely protective of your meditation space and time. This in and of itself is a great exercise in installing a nonnegotiable habit for *you.*

9. *Memorialize your commitment.*
Be the architect of your "commitment statement" in a way that specifically captures your promise to yourself. For example, you might write:

Beginning Monday, August 29, I will install a meditation practice by sitting in my meditation space on time and every day at 6:15 a.m. for one full minute, over a period of two consecutive weeks. My intention is to sit still, not only for the benefit of myself but ultimately the benefit of all. I endeavor to extend the duration of my practice as it develops and becomes stronger. I will continue titration until I reach the timing that is best for me. I am open to and trust in the process. Deo volente. God willing.

10. *Let it rip! Bring it on!*
You now have access to the basics you'll need to install this new practice of regularly getting still. Or perhaps you're renewing an older practice by getting a bit more serious about it.

Wherever you are on this journey of practicing stillness, beware of the temptation to think about how you have witnessed others "meditating" in the past, what they looked like, and what you are supposed to look like, do, and not do. Let go of any preconceived notions you may have about meditation and its "requirements."

The Tibetan word for meditation is "gom" or "gohm," meaning "to become familiar with your mind." When we sit, we become familiar with our minds. But we also get to know our own minds when we place our attention on a piece of music, look at a flower or tree, read something that is inspirational, or even notice a chest pain.

Getting to know our own mind looks different for everyone because it *is* different for everyone. So please be open to and genuine with the practice of becoming familiar with your mind. It might feel weird or awkward because it is new to you. So likely did every other new thing you ever tried for the first time. But it doesn't matter what the practice is called or how silly it may seem. It only matters that you show up for yourself, as yourself, authentically and consistently.

Four

Steppingstone #2: Equanimity
The Intentional Act of Welcoming Everything

<u>Merriam-Webster definition</u>
Equanimity: "Evenness of mind especially under stress"

<u>Healing Path definition</u>
Equanimity: "Making space in our lives for all the parts of us, even the broken ones"

Not only was "equanimity" a new word for my vocabulary, but it was also a new way of being. Don't stop reading if the word or concept is completely foreign. This steppingstone is too powerful to skip. By the end of this chapter, you will learn practical ways to employ this concept in daily life.

The concept of equanimity may be the single most impactful variable that has helped me transition from constantly reaching for armor to protect myself to moving into a space where I no longer need to defend myself at all. Equanimity means saying "yes" to everything. It means removing the turnstile at the gate of our minds, the turnstile that works relentlessly to regulate what gets in and fights so hard to keep out certain things (like grief and pain).

Equanimity arises when we make the decision to stop seeking pleasure and stop avoiding pain. We release the need to control circumstance after potential circumstance. We have been clinging to a blanket of conditional acceptance by systematically deciding which parts of ourselves and the world are allowed to be here. With equanimity, we remove the "picking and choosing" stage of the process and intentionally choose to let our whole selves, and the whole world, all be here together. It is the most challenging and also the most liberating mental shift I have ever made.

What equanimity is *not*. Allowing ourselves to be in situations that are unsafe. Becoming a passive victim and exposing ourselves to things we know are not in our best interests with a dismissive, helpless spirit of "It is what it is." Handing over our authentic power with an attitude of "I can't do anything right anyway."

What equanimity *is*. Surrender. The exhale to replace all exhales. A relinquishing of the need to pick and choose what is real. The dissolving of whatever limiting lenses we have been seeing the world through to serve our egos. An awareness that all things are transient and that we can live more peacefully when we can train ourselves to remain open to the comings and goings of all experiences.

When we give permission for everything to be here, we find that we, too, are included in that allotment. We tame the compulsive need constantly to "fix" ourselves and others. We quit our relentless habit of trying to validate our existence. We open to all of life, come what may. We let go of the false narratives we tell ourselves. We start learning to catch ourselves, one judgment at a time. We transition from criticism and contraction to acceptance and opening.

Embracing this concept of equanimity can ignite an energy shift away from always trying to play small, protect ourselves or to preplan how to fend off sneak attacks by grief, guilt, or shame. We move instead to focusing our energy solely on what is here, now.

I recall an example of my own experience with this energy shift when I was learning to play golf many years ago. At the time, I did not have a stillness practice and probably employed few if any of the principles I am now describing in this book. I was shopping with my mother to purchase a golf club bag. Once I found the style I liked, I reached for the black one.

Mom saw my color choice and immediately said, *What about this red one, Lisa? Or this pink one? This is pretty.*

After she asked a second time, I responded, *No, thanks. Black is good. I am not trying to draw attention to myself.*

Why not? Mom asked.

Ugh. My heart instantly started aching, and my stomach turned into a sludge of hot anxiety lava that felt like it would drown me right there at the store. My face turned a deep, hot red. Just thinking about it today makes my heart rate jump and skip.

I stood my ground. *The black one works. Let's go.*

I couldn't answer Mom's question then, but I didn't let it go. I have been thinking about her question all of these years since. And I realize that today I actually can answer her question of *Why not?*

Why didn't I want to draw attention to myself? The difference in feeling capable of adequately responding to her question is underpinned by the energy shift I have experienced as a result of embracing equanimity. It has allowed me to build perspective. Before this energy shift and during that long emotionally numb season that took up over half my life, I was relentlessly terrorized by my grief. I was imprisoned by the threat of its power and the fear that it could surface and overtake me at any time. It could erupt in the most unlikely of situations, such as shopping for a golf bag.

I was self-conscious, self-absorbed, and scared almost all of the time. I could only see things through the panic and threat of exposure. Fear ruled me and kept me silent about my grief. As unchecked fear can do, it bubbled over into other areas of my life, and I stopped showing up anywhere (not just the driving range) so I wouldn't risk being seen. I couldn't bear the thought of anyone looking at me because I was afraid they might actually see all the pain I was carrying. I thought that if the depths of my pain were to truly express themselves, maybe they would scare everyone away. They certainly scared me. But until recently, those depths of pain have been imprisoned and harnessed. Without the strength to depend on myself no matter what, I have been too intimidated to show up and be seen.

Standing guard all of the time, I was always looking around for the next emotional assault and trying to dodge it or get ahead of it. So I tried constantly to blend in, move along, go with the flow, and choose black over red or pink whenever possible. I didn't want anyone to know about or notice the muddy painful sludge bubble that invisibly engulfed my entire being as I safely (or so I thought moved through those days and years of my life.

Not wanting to draw attention to oneself can be one of the very subtle but toxic side effects of unattended grief. The golf bag is an example of just how insidious grief can be. One minute we are choosing a black golf bag because we want to blend in and the next we end up getting to the point where we hide so deeply and darkly that eventually there is no color in anything we feel, see, do, or have. Fear expands, our worlds contract, and over time we not only isolate ourselves from others to increase our sense of protection, but we also disengage from any real connection with our true selves for the same reason.

Embracing the stepping stone of equanimity changed all of that for me. The energy shifted. Not quickly. Not overtly. But over time, I have learned to reprogram my mind and heart not just to tolerate but to sincerely invite the entire surround of my experience to be part of my awareness. And while this has sometimes felt excruciating and at other times I have been ecstatic, acceptance of the invitation has helped me to reconnect with my soul (sole) self.

Equanimity has opened a space for me to explore, for myself, which colors I like and which ones I don't. I have developed a better sense of when I want to be seen and when I want privacy.

I am learning the difference between fear and excitement. I regularly experience deep joy. I also experience raging, emotional wounds that turn into somatic physical pain. But it is all allowed to be here. That is the power of equanimity and an example of how the energy shift can happen.

Thanksgiving dinner is another time I have felt this shift in energy. For at least two decades, I have been making Thanksgiving dinners, celebrating this holiday with a house full of people, spending hundreds of dollars in provisions to feed us all for the four-day weekend, and cleaning up before, during, and after the festivities.

Hosting big Thanksgiving dinners and opening our home to many loved ones is something I have enjoyed to my core. We have our annual traditions, including participating in what we call the "Gratitude Circle." This tradition is a pre-feast circle that is formed as each person holds a candle. I usually lead the candle lighting with the candle we lit when our daughter, Alexis, was baptized at Children's National Medical Center in Washington, D.C., just two months before her death in 1997.

The circle starts when I light that candle, share what I am grateful for, then help the next person in the circle light their candle from mine. Each person shares a reflection if they want, and soon we are standing in a circle of light and gratitude. Participants range from young to old. The experience is powerful.

The final candle in the circle is held by Ernest, the father of our children, who holds the one we lit for our son Emmanuel, who died at birth in 2002. Once the circle of lighted candles is completed, we send our thanks out into the world and place the lit candles all around on tables and counters throughout the kitchen and dining room to stay flickering throughout the meal. It's beautiful. This is just one of the things I love about hosting Thanksgiving!

But a couple of years ago, we changed our tradition. We went to my mother's house out of state. She declined our offers to bring, make, or do anything to help. This was awesome, as we had traveled over a thousand miles to get there! We literally showed up to a delicious meal in a stunning setting. All of my energy went into being present.

Unlike all the Thanksgiving dinners I had prepared over the years, on this day I wasn't exhausted and half asleep. I wasn't running through the checklist in my mind of all the things that still needed my attention. I wasn't planning when the stove should be on or off, how to keep the food warm, or whether someone had spilled wine on the carpet.

I was just there, in gratitude, experiencing the people and the food there as if it were the only meal I would ever have again. I delighted in each moment—the hustle and bustle of Mom's kitchen, the smells of the food, and the connection with our family and friends. I left all my emotional baggage at the door and simply arrived in the moments that constituted that day.

Practicing equanimity does not mean that I no longer wish to host Thanksgiving feasts or only hope to go to someone else's house for that important meal. It doesn't mean I sat through that recent

Thanksgiving dinner at my mother's house in silence and checked out of the company and conversation.

It means that when I choose to host Thanksgiving dinner, I am learning to worry less about logistics and more about how to be there and experience the day. It means that when I go to someone else's home, I actually show up and engage. I aim to consciously stay open to all of it over and over again. And with enough practice, the choice point of whether to stress or whether to just be present and allow it all to be as is falls away. I begin to automatically skip the middleman and go right toward building the new habit of being present rather than fearful (disguised as stress) without even realizing it. The result is that I am able to more consistently show up as myself, instead of as the muted, scared, terrorized version of myself.

When we embrace equanimity, we allow everything to be as it is without labeling it "good" or "bad." We let go of our likes and dislikes. We still have preferences, but they are not part of our identity. The mental, emotional, and physical energy required from us to constantly manage this tug-of-war between whether we should stay numb or show up loses its momentum as we stop trying to control, resist, hide, cover, and run from pain. Our energy is then available for other experiences, like actually participating in the events of our lives instead of just trying to survive them. In this way, we move to thriving.

So how do we begin to practice equanimity and try to bring about a more open existence? Can there actually be any type of relief from suffering after a miscarriage and the deaths of two children? Though shocking even still to me, my experience tells me that yes, there can be relief. But it is not a natural eventuality. Time does not heal all wounds. As with any new activity we want to learn, we have to actively and intentionally choose to practice equanimity and build our skills moment to moment, indefinitely.

As humans, our natural inclination is *not* to accept things as they are, so why should we bother learning about this concept? Well, what if we ceased our constant stream of opinions and judgments and just opened? What if we could release our mental training of wanting things to be different than they are? What if we could participate in our lives, instead of just tolerating them? If these transitions are at all possible, I think they begin to unfold when we take a break from our safety armor and start to become open-hearted, exposed, and vulnerable. Doing this allows us to settle into a (perhaps foreign sense of "okayness." In this very moment, there is nowhere to go. Nothing to do. No one to fix, least of all ourselves.

Pursuing equanimity also provides respite for ourselves. When grieving, we become chronically depleted of energy. We are working, working, working to keep the whole facade up so we can hide. The older we get, the more opinions we form about what we like and what we don't.

This exhaustion shows up in the form of rules and phrases about what we "do" and "don't do' during the course of our everyday lives. Food is an easy illustration. Having rules in place removes required decision-making energy from our proverbial plates. The surplus of food that has been available in this part of the world has allowed us to get very particular about what we eat, when, how, and why. Have you cooked dinner for a group of people lately? Good luck getting it right.

The key element of the equanimity practice is to recognize our tendency to brace against certain things in our environments so we can learn to let the choice not to brace emerge. Discovering how this happens in our physical bodies is a helpful step toward understanding what is possible in our ways of thinking and living.

For example, you may have back pain or the phone may be ringing or the kids might be hollering outside your bedroom door. But when practicing equanimity, we say yes to all of it—even if just for a moment. When we do this, we get a whiff of the all-encompassing, pervasive relief of what life would be like if we could learn to open and allow everything to be as it is.

Please note, I strongly encourage you to create some type of stillness practice before delving into the discovery of equanimity. While both disciplines share a lot in common, I do not recommend trying to partake in both of these practices for the first time simultaneously, as it could be a traumatic combination.

The difference between stillness and equanimity is that meditation is stillness itself. Equanimity can be cultivated during periods of stillness, but it is not a passive manifestation. It is more intentional than that. It is a permission we grant ourselves in that moment. We choose to say "yes" to whatever is happening around us and resist the habit of bracing against anything.

Both stillness and equanimity require significant practice and perhaps professional support. You will need all the courage you can muster just to learn how to sit still before stepping into the equanimity quest. But once you're there, you will be ready to give this a try. And you guessed it: just like sitting still, it's not complicated, but it ain't easy.

ature; *Practical Application: Everyday Equanimity*

Of the ten stepping stones, this may be the most challenging to implement, as it is not a concept familiar to most people. Below are some practical application actions you can experiment with. The idea is to pick one or two actions, start layering them into your daily life, and then noticing your experience of choosing to say yes to whatever is happening right now, instead of habitually and selectively resisting life.

Equanimity is complex, and there are endless informational resources available for your own discovery. For the purpose of getting introduced, I suggest trying one action below to see if you can actually experience even one moment of letting everything be as it is. We are getting to know the essence and the feeling of that moment so that we can recognize and cultivate additional such moments more easily. That is the magic we can create.

1. *Notice your preferences.*
   We all have likes and dislikes. Next time you are about to form an opinion that you don't like something and if you are inclined to act in response to your dislike, stop yourself from acting just for a moment. Notice what narratives you are telling yourself. Then jump into the

actual moment and test your ability to refrain from making an adjustment to "fix" your dislike. This could look something like this.

> *I am cold. I need to turn up the heat. This car is freezing. Why does the driver have to keep the car so cold? He knows how cold I get.*

P A U S E.

At the moment where you would normally comment to express your discomfort or reach to turn up the shared heat source in the vehicle, you wait. You do nothing. You realize being cold or hot is not a problem—it is just a condition.

A C T.

Perhaps you still do the reflexive action of complaining or changing the car temperature. But as you become comfortable with getting curious about things, you may also begin to challenge that reflexive action with a different reaction. This might look something like the following.

> *I am cold. I need to turn up the heat. This car is freezing. Why does the driver have to keep the car so cold? He knows how cold I get.*

Instead of reacting without thinking, pause and do nothing. Just notice your inclination to complain or to reach for the console and turn up the heat. And then don't complain or turn up the heat.

Instead, check in with yourself:
> *Oops! There I go again telling myself stories. I am cold, but I can just as easily put my jacket on instead of trying to immediately change the entire environment or complaining aloud. If I don't warm up after that, I will ask my partner if he would please turn the heat up a bit.*

Learning to notice our preferences allows us to choose our reactions to things more intentionally, instead of being on autopilot, forgetting that there are others in the car and that we are not the only ones who want to be comfortable. This noticing creates a space for everything to be as it is and an opportunity to make a decision about what is truly the best way to address an unwanted condition or circumstance.

When you become very practiced at this, you will start to notice your preference, but instead of automatically responding to it, you may choose to do nothing and conclude that being a little chilly isn't a problem after all.

2. *Allow others to finish speaking before crafting your response and/or interrupting.*
Oh, this is so hard to do! But it is an interesting way to access the present moment and allow things to be as they are. Generally speaking when we are in conversation, we somewhat listen to the words of another while

simultaneously preparing what we will say next. Sometimes we can't wait.

Sometimes our compulsive needs to be seen and heard cause us to forget our manners, and we interrupt one another. The experiment here is to try allowing someone you are chatting with to just keep talking until they are finished. You may be surprised to learn that there is usually more to what the person is saying than we give them time to express.

A more evolved version of this specific action is to consciously choose to be the last one in a group conversation to share your input. When we are in groups, we tend to compete for airtime. When a question is asked and we feel we have the fastest and best response in the room, we jump into this competition, often without even realizing it. There can be great benefit to allowing others to speak first and holding your response back until others have commented, especially in groups. Give it a shot!

3. *Yield to a car trying to pull in front of you, even if the other driver doesn't have the right of way or have a signal on.*
Traffic is congested. There are more distractions than ever. Populations are dense and moving in every direction. It seems there is always some driver trying to get the advantage on the highway and even local roads. Next time that happens, instead of getting annoyed at someone trying to jump in front of your vehicle, pause. Try to refrain from telling yourself a narrative about that

vehicle and its passengers. Just let them through and be okay with it. No stories. No resentment. As you look for opportunities to practice and do this often, you may also notice you, too, are being let into traffic by kind souls more often than you used to be.

4. *Thank someone for something. Full stop.*
So often when someone does something for us, we thank them, but we add our caveats. This can look something like this: *Thanks for the ride. I can't believe my car broke down again. It's so annoying. I wish I could afford a more reliable car. I guess it's just not in the cards right now.*

The suggestion here is that we try to catch and stop ourselves from using gratitude disguised as a platform for complaints. Try just saying thank you and smiling at the person. Let the shared space of appreciation dangle without adding more words. Allow your gratitude to stand independently of carving it up. For example, you might say, *Thanks for the ride, I sincerely appreciate your help today.*

When we use qualifiers in our gratitude, we tend to shift the focus away from the appreciation for the individual who did us a kindness and onto ourselves and our own issues. We don't have to say everything we are thinking. We just need to say "thank you" and let that stand as the expression of our gratitude. In this way, we are letting things be as they are, without secretly hoping that person feels a little sorry for us because our car doesn't run properly.

Equanimity is about letting everything be here. You may wish you had a better car, but that is your problem, and there is no merit in adding self-pitying comments. Doing so tends to diffuse the spirit of our intended gratitude and has the potential to dilute the appreciation we sincerely do feel and wish to convey.

5. *Resist the thousands of daily urges to look at your smart phone. Or resist even once.*
Because we are addicted to our smart devices, we have endless, built-in chances each day to pause and allow things to be as they are. The action is completely self-explanatory.

Try to catch yourself before acting on the thought of checking your phone for texts, emails, and alerts. Our devices are chronically hijacking our time and attention for multiple hours every day. I am not suggesting that we ignore them. But I think we can agree that there is a difference between times when there is a genuine need for the phone and communication and other moments when we are just bored or nervous and need to fill our idle time. When we are engaged with electronics, equanimity is not possible, let alone even in the same zip code as we are. Pausing to discern whether there is actually a need to check our devices before we enter our passwords is a simple way to catch our habitual patterns and look at what is here.

An advanced version of this specific action is to consciously choose to restrict access to your phone during certain periods of the day. I have heard this referred to as a digital sunset. Several years ago, I started implementing my own evening shutdown. More recently, I have structured my digital sunsets in ways that let silence actually be my default. This means that I have implemented times for my phone to be on in my environment rather than the default being on and having to turn it off.

This is a powerful tool because we have these practice opportunities arise naturally without us having to look for or create them. Waiting even a second or two before reaching for our device allows space for us to make an informed decision. We can decide if we actually *need* to check something or if we are just uncomfortable with the quiet space, we might find ourselves in. Perhaps we just don't feel comfortable with our brains being in roaming mode. Challenge your habit of repeatedly turning to your device, and notice what it feels like to override that habit. Equanimity is always here, waiting to be embraced instead of escaped.

6. *Learn to become aware of the statements you make that box you into rigidity.*
Phrases like "I always" and "I never" are limiting. They do not leave any room for an outcome other than the one you are predicting, creating, and maybe even demanding. When we use an all-encompassing statement to draw a line in the sand, we may feel a sense of protection. However, when we draw those big bright lines, we also kill any potential for nuance or any outcome other than

the one we have declared. We might say *I always take this route to work,* or *I never go that way.*

Enter the Waze app. Waze is an everyday exercise in equanimity. This driving navigation app allows you to enter your departure and destination locations so it can run its algorithms to identify the most direct route available. Waze takes into account real-time traffic patterns, accidents, outages, and other factors we can't see so that it can tell us the best way to go. We might respond like this: *Weird. I wonder where this route goes. I don't think I have tried this way. Let's give the algorithms a shot at giving me the best route, instead of doing what I "always" do and turn here. What have I got to lose?*

Waze identifies the causes and conditions of the various relevant roads that are currently underway without care for history or future. Waze does not include a narrative to "always" or "never" adopt a certain route. Equanimity (via Waze) gives you options to consider, and unencumbered by habit and reflective action, you can choose the best route for that moment in time. Maybe you'd rather be on slower back roads without so much traffic even if the distance is greater. Or maybe you are making a phone call, and you'd rather sit still in the traffic of a main highway so you can be more engaged with your conversation.

The point is this: Because you're not rigidly wed to "always" or "never" choosing certain routes, the landscape of possibilities opens, and you can choose the best one with the information you have *in that moment*, even if the route you choose this time is different than the one you took last time. Making decisions in real time by opening to all of the options, considering the current landscape, and acting in the face of these ever-changing elements is equanimity in action.

7. *Eat something prepared for you exactly as it is served.*
Especially in the West, we have a surplus of food (or food-like substances—not everything we eat qualifies as nutritious). This has allowed us to become very picky eaters. We not only have preferences, but we also have rules. Some of us have even made a religion out of our food.

These rules may be tied up in spiritual dogma. Or they may have arisen from legitimate medical issues. Our taste buds, habits, and limiting rules about what we each eat as individuals have skyrocketed because food surplus allows us that luxury. But such an endless array of food choices can be a curse when it results in our belief that we need to have things made and served the way we want or perhaps even the way we require. Always.

Don't get me wrong. I am the first person at a restaurant to ask the kitchen to "hold" something I don't like or to "add" an extra helping of things I do like. You probably do this also, even if you don't realize it. But when we repeatedly customize our food orders, we are not practicing equanimity because we are controlling our environment to make ourselves more comfortable and to please our palates.

There is a time and place for all things, including when we want a salad made to our specifications. This is not the problem. The problem only arises when we get so rigid that we can't have it any other way (again, we are not talking about medical conditions). Rigidity like this causes our worlds to shrink, diminishing the spaces where we feel safe (or satiated). The more we indulge our preferences, the fewer places we feel at home.

Try accessing equanimity by ordering something from a menu "as is" and not customizing it by "holding" some ingredient or requesting some component of the order be placed on the side.

See if you can pick around the things you don't like, instead of seeing them as a threat to your enjoyment and nourishment. Try to do this silently, without explanation or conversation with others about it. Explore what it's like for the salad to be okay as it is. This activity is a metaphor for recognizing equanimity so we can develop our practice and apply it far beyond something as arbitrary as food.

Another easy time to try this experiment is when someone other than you cooks. When is the last time you consumed a home-cooked meal prepared by hands other than yours, simply ate what was there, and said thank you instead of qualifying it or adding your preferences? Or alternatively how often might you prepare and serve a meal to a handful of people without at least one or two giving you their menu requirements before, during, and after the meal?

I am not suggesting we eat things to be polite per se, certainly not all of the time. But periodically choosing to keep our food preferences to ourselves is a way to bring awareness to our idiosyncratic requirements, which in this case are applied to food. Equanimity is about noticing everything in this moment, whether we love it or think it's disgusting, without letting what we notice drive us into reactive action without the awareness that most of our self-imposed rules, around what we eat and otherwise, are organically self-generated.

Never should we do something that we perceive to be "bad" for us (although many of us tend to eat substances that are demonstrated to threaten our health). However, the list of foods and beverages we have decided are "bad" for us or what we "always" eat or "never" drink is usually just that—a list we have made up. We have created a limiting set of beliefs and all-or-nothing rules about food that quite frankly have caused us to forget our respectful and gracious manners when dining out or with others.

If we consciously make a decision that we cannot eat something, we can just say "no thank you" without adding our defense strategy to it. If we want more of something, we can ask for that, too. What reveals our equanimity in the moment is the act of noticing our likes and dislikes, not the labels we assign to them. Everything is allowed to be here as is. We can learn to navigate our preferences without having to share them with others.

8. *Let the music play.*
   This is another easy, cost-free, and fast way to tap into equanimity. I am a music lover and almost always have some type of music playing. I enjoy so many different types of music. Sometimes guest listeners marvel at the abrupt transitions in my playlists from gospel to Led Zeppelin, jazz to the Indigo Girls, and almost every other type of music I can find. I am ever grateful that my ears function well so I can enjoy listening to anything and everything.

   Between SiriusXM, Spotify, Pandora, Apple Music, and my own library, it becomes very easy to skip the stuff I don't feel like hearing and continue scrolling until a song I "like" is found. There is nothing inherently wrong with skipping songs we don't want to hear.

   But next time you have the itch to change stations or skip some tune, try to tap into the equanimity that is always here, always free, always waiting for us to show up in the current moment. By "tap into," I am suggesting that, again, instead of reacting unconsciously by skipping to the next song, we *pause* and recognize that we have a choice but don't necessarily need to make it. We might say to ourselves, *Dang, I have always kind of hated this song. Everyone loves it. I guess it's a "classic," but it's never been my thing. My inclination is to skip it, but do I really need to, or am I just in the habit when it comes to this particular song?*

What happens next is actually of little importance. As long as we learn to practice pausing before habitually and unconsciously reacting, we have tapped into the current moment and made the best choice given our circumstances. Some days I will skip that "classic" song anyway because I really don't like it and don't want to hear it. But every once in a while, I turn it up louder to see if I can appreciate it the way others do. I allow myself to experience it firsthand and then decide what, if any, action is appropriate.

9. *Be last to let go of someone in the course of a hug.*
   Try this one today! Hug your friend, partner, child, family member, or whomever you might hug in the course of a day. Only this time, pay attention to the hug itself. Instead of rotely leaning in and going through the motions as if it were just another transaction, see if you can stay in that embrace until the other person releases it, rather than being the one to pull away.

   Obviously, this is a much more intimate and personal way to experiment with giving up control in order to be present to what is here, now. But it is also an effective and easy exercise to try. Pay particular attention to see if you are able to let the person you presumably care about enough to embrace their physical body decide when the hug has concluded or if you have to hold onto that control and pull away first.

Here again, we are practicing the intentional pause which is the essence of equanimity. We ask ourselves: *What's here? Do I really need to act? Will everyone survive if I am* not *the one in control?*

10. *Physically ground yourself.*
Finally, a comfy and physical way to introduce yourself to this concept is to lie down on the ground, floor, carpet, mat, or wherever you find yourself in a safe and secure place to play with this idea. But it must be the ground you lie down on (even if there are carpets). No beds or couches—get as low to the ground as you can. If you are in an environment where you can be on the actual physical ground that is Mother Earth, even better!

When you lie down on your back, facing upward in the supine position, move and extend your arms and legs just a little bit away from your body. Open your palms so they face upward, and take a couple of breaths. Settle into the feeling of being secure on the ground. Then see if you can say yes literally and/or mentally to everything in your sense perception.

As you lie on your back and face the sky (or the ceiling and indirectly the sky), imagine that every element of your physical experience is welcome. The temperature of the air, the hungry belly, the noisy lawnmower outside, your lists of things to do, the breath you breathe in, the breath you breathe out—they are all welcome here.

We are so used to the efficiency of our brains thinking of two, three, four, or twenty decisions up the tree of possible outcomes to make sure we are not caught off guard. But the truth is that most of those twenty decisions may never come to pass. We spend so much mental energy in hypotheticals that we miss what's in front of us.

Lying on the ground in the supine position for even one minute can create the space for you to tap into the equanimity, the "it's-all-okay-to-be-here" essence, that is already present.

That is a quick look at some ways you can get familiar with this concept of equanimity. As you may have noticed, the key element of this stepping stone is the pause. Each of the ten steps described is just a different way to pause in the midst of our actions and make sure we are making decisions with current information, instead of habitually reacting to or relying on an opinion or belief we formed decades ago.

Ultimately, the magic we seek here is to see what it would be like to just say "yes" instead of trying to control every aspect of our lives and what is coming next. As long-time grievers, we may find it natural to fall into patterns of attempts at excessive control in response to our injuries. But we can take these patterns too far. If we don't pause and check in with what's here, we miss most of life because we are already planning our responses. As we plan in anticipation of what could happen next, we tend to narrate those plans that are days and weeks and sometimes years out from right now.

The best description of equanimity that I have heard is "The Big Okay." Practicing equanimity starts by saying okay to little things like letting a car in front of us or resisting the need to complain and share each one of our personal annoyances and physical ailments with those around us. We begin where we are, letting someone else release the hug before we do or allowing someone to fully finish speaking before we craft and share a response.

When we practice equanimity in the smallest of ways but with intentional consistency and curiosity, it can evolve into a life-changing shift in thinking as it did for me. As with all lasting change, this shift occurs subtly and at its own pace. But as we develop our skills through practice and by choosing to see what it feels like to let things be as they are, that shift is inevitable.

What does the equanimity shift feel like? It feels like being on an airplane about to land, when the wheels underneath us cautiously, then completely touch the ground of a landing pad and the pilot concludes the plane's journey. It feels like Friday evening at five o'clock when no matter what work awaits us on Saturday morning, the majority of the demands placed on us through our work and personal schedules temporarily abate for the evening. It feels like waking up to the smell of freshly brewed coffee, even when we aren't coffee drinkers. We still like it because it's soothing. It feels familiar. It feels safe. We know that aroma personally. We crave more experiences of our world feeling soothed, familiar, and safe. And these experiences are available to us.

Always here, always free, always infinite, always waiting to be integrated, equanimity is patient and able to bring peace into our rigid, armored world. We practice equanimity with one small intention, one small choice at a time, like trying the practical application experiments. We do this knowing the shift is underway. We choose this because we understand that this is the path to spaciousness and calm abiding. We do so with the knowledge that although we have already tried every single other approach to find our way home, we still feel lost. Equanimity is the way home.

Five

Steppingstone #3: Observation What's Here?

<u>Merriam-Webster definition</u>
Observe: "To come to realize or know especially through consideration of noted facts"

<u>Healing Path definition</u>
Observe: "Backing out of our preprogrammed, narrow views of everything and routinely looking around with fresh eyes and a childlike curiosity"

Once we lay some foundational pavers, like getting still and then saying yes to our emerging experience instead of bracing against it and labeling everything, we are ready to cultivate an authentic curiosity about what this life actually is. We look around, but for the first time in a long time, and maybe for the first time ever, we are not interpreting, judging, narrating, and planning. Observation is about pulling back the curtains we have strategically hung to create the environment we thought we wanted and actually seeing what is there—independent of putting our personal spin on things.

Unlike the first two pavers of stillness and equanimity, you are probably familiar with the general definition of observation and are also likely practiced at it. But I invite you to let go of the observation techniques you have honed thus far. I suggest you try to fall back out of the indoctrination we have all experienced. By indoctrination, I am referring to the countless ways we have trained our minds to constantly judge, take inventory, and time travel by focusing on the past or rushing into the future.

We have been taught to observe with a critical eye. We have learned that most of the time when we observe, it is for comparison purposes or functional opportunities. We rarely observe for the innate delight of taking in an item or situation. We don't see things as they are. We fall far short of experiencing the full glorious surround of imagery and situations because we only see things from our own perspective, with our personal (and usually unchallenged narrative playing again and again in our fixed, efficient minds.

Until the last few years, most of the observation techniques I learned and became skilled at performing had little to do with healing. These techniques were born from the need to survive by rationalizing my choices and justifying my actions. Once I started cultivating a different type of observation technique, my narrow view cracked wide open. What a splendid surprise! It's the type of dynamic we don't know we are missing until we get a taste of the good stuff.

How do we make the transition? In the context of healing, the type of observation we work to cultivate is an organic effort to quiet ourselves so we can see with fresh eyes. The images are crisper and more alive. The lens I look through now encompasses more than just my own limited view, based on personal experience, demographics, and dogma. My now panoramic lens is in wide focus and includes more as I continue to practice. More of what I observe is actually visible. More of what I imagine starts to seem possible.

Before I discuss the "how" of observation, I want to first establish what "good" looks like in applying this different technique of observation. I love this stepping stone because it is so easy to point to the illustration that speaks most loudly. Turn to a young child or a pet to take note of the elements that constitute this type of undistracted observation.

When an underdeveloped, not-yet-mind-trained child sees something for the first time, he or she approaches it with a nonpresumptuous curiosity. Even if the child has seen an object before, he or she still pays it fresh attention, moves it around, tries to taste it, feel it, and even see how far the item can be thrown. Children take in the world with all of their senses. Their experience of life is not blocked by outdated conclusions and tainted critical eyes, which work so hard to make what they are looking at fit in a preconstructed framework. This preconstruction is what happens with age if we are not careful.

When we engage with pets, they, too, embody what it means to curiously observe. Next time you sit down and pet your dog or cat, lock eyeballs with them, then see if you can notice the question marks that form the backdrop of their expression. It's subtle. But it is consistent. When things come into focus and you recognize this quality of nonpresumptuous curiosity, you now have a powerful example of what it means to simply observe.

Kids and pets don't attach all of their personal baggage from the last million times they observed something to the view they currently hold. They don't judge their view as "good" or "bad" until they have been trained and also expected to do so. Once again, we see the recurring theme: this stepping stone is simple but not easy.

Like all of these practices, observation takes courage. Clear observation is not a new place we hang out all the time. It is a collection of glimpses we are willing to take now that we have slowed down and stopped trying to predict and control everything. These glimpses can be excruciatingly painful. If we have never let ourselves truly look around, we may take a peek at our surroundings and find ourselves wanting to run for the hills.

In fact, it is likely that when the lights first come on, we will turn them off. We may have been enthusiastic about getting out of the proverbial briar patch. But until we build a life in a new space that feels safe, warm, and loving, we can feel displaced, like we don't fit anywhere.

My personal journey with observation is that I turned the lights on and off for about twenty-five years before I found the bravery to just leave them on. I have found this to be true no matter how much time has passed since loss occurred.

Whether we hung those blinder curtains so we only had to observe selective reality a day ago or a decade ago, our instinct may still be to pull them shut. That is okay. Think of it as a reverse indicator that you are now within the zip code of clear observation's geography. The more you want to run, the more you know you are on the path home to yourself.

We don't start our healing path with observation. We must first practice learning to get still and learning to say yes with equanimity. Building those foundational muscles will help us through this next step of trying to get a glimpse of what is actually here—not just what we have been programmed to see and what we have worked so hard to explain and protect.

We may be scared by what we observe: heartbreak, tragedy, isolation, emptiness, anger, fury, resentment, guilt, shame, sadness, longing, aching, helplessness, apathy, even desperation. But there is no threat in our practice of observation. We improve our vision, so to speak, without submerging ourselves in the feelings that scare us. We see them, and they are real. But the more we practice observation, the more our propensity to judge, have opinions, and label emotions we feel as "good" and "bad" slowly falls away,

Like stillness and equanimity practices, we do this in small doses. A slow pace may be required if what we observe is too debilitating and overwhelming for us to bear. We may seek the support of a trusted friend, therapist, coach, guru, or clergy member to stand by us as we navigate this courageous willingness to look at what is really here. We may want to start a journal, a photography habit, or video diary to help us process what we find.

Unbridled observation can feel so threatening that we may initially run off this path by stuffing ourselves with anesthesia like food, alcohol, retail therapy—or "fill in the blank with your favorite numbing agent." If and when this happens, we let *that* be here, too.

Remember, with observation we don't judge or resist. We just show up and let ourselves notice what's here. It is natural to step into and out of observing again and again. This ongoing cycle actually constitutes the observation practice itself.

As with all practices, our skills improve over time. We don't have to move into this new space permanently: it may be more of a room we ease into when we know we have the support we will need to tolerate and process what we find. In the beginning, we may notice little sparks of clear moments. Eventually these flickering teaser moments can be developed into minutes, hours, days, weeks, and a lifetime of "real seeing." Before we know it, observation becomes a skill we are not only good at but also one we enjoy and rely upon.

By now, you may be thinking, *No way! Not a chance! I'm not interested in seeing what's here. It's too hard. I will suffocate and die if I sit with my pain.*

You may be right about that. But I have worn lots of crafty lenses since my daughter died twenty-five years ago, and they did not lead me to myself. My tinted lenses merely postponed my understanding of the little-known fact that when it comes to patience, our grief has us beat every time.

Grief can outlast any storm, blaze through the thickest of tinted lenses, and hang tight until we decide to choose observation. In my experience, most people will *not* choose to observe due to their fear. This fear is real. We are scared because we have tasted grief. It has evolved out of the exposure we have already gleaned: grief can be torturous and at times intolerable to our senses mentally, physically, and emotionally. No one else can decide for us if this is a risk we can afford to take and whether or not we personally have the courage to take it.

Even as you feel a quiet longing for something else and even as you know at your core that there has to be some alternate, more enlivened way to exist, you may turn those lights off and conclude that you can already see clearly enough. Perhaps you got your hands on some very thick, very flashy, very seductive, and also very dependable proverbially tinted lenses, and they are working just fine, thank you.

The decision to practice observation is a profound and intentional choice that each of us can make. Personally, my tinted lenses worked just fine until about five years ago. I kicked and screamed, ingested substances that rendered me unable to feel anything at all, and ran as fast and as far as I could (as I literally became a marathon runner) until there was no more choosing.

For me, this choice became a matter of survival. I was suffocating myself with all the different numbing agents I could access to avoid looking at my losses. Although I had no "vision" of what else was possible, I realized that the festering pain was actually leading me further into an unending mode of self-destruction.

So I made a conscious decision to lean into the practice of observation. Frightened, bruised, and scarred, I took the risk. Because the lenses couldn't shield me forever. After so many years of struggling not to see, I burned out from the energy it took to avoid it all.

But there is hope on the horizon! It was through taking that risk (again and again and again that I discovered this: once I learned to get still, say yes to what is here, and intentionally observe it, there was more than sheer pain pulling at my shirt sleeve for attention.

Yes, as I became more present, mountains of unchecked pain I'd run from were waiting for me. When I broke open the locked crates that were holding my deepest, darkest feelings about loss and my anger, regret, guilt, and resentment, those crates burst open. Horrifying feelings came rushing out as if they couldn't wait one more moment to take a breath.

Partnering with a trusted advisor during this process is critical. When the initial storm hits, we need support. We need safety. We need connection. We need community. When the flood of pain reaches the tidal wave status, we may be paralyzed by fear. We may be so full of rage we want to drive our car off a cliff and be done.

But mountains of unchecked pain are not all that I found as I learned to observe! Allowing my senses to run wild, free from tainted barriers, I found that other cool things to observe like forgiveness, self-compassion, and confidence were also tugging at my shirt sleeve. I observed energy, meaning, and direction. I found unbridled clarity, self-respect, and creativity. We think we are barricading the "pain" with our tinted lenses and other obstacles, but we don't realize we cannot selectively numb our emotions.

When we dull the pain, we dull the love, too. We either feel it all, or we don't. Choosing not to feel is like drawing a blanket of Bubble Wrap around ourselves. The blanket doesn't sport a logo that says *Pain, go away, but if you are here to let the good times roll, c'mon in.* The logo just says *Keep life out!* In other words, our experience of life is that we feel safest when we numb everything and feel nothing. Feeling nothing, neither pain nor ecstasy, is a flagrant waste of our ability to experience everything! Our human potential to feel everything is unfulfilled in those of us who have decided it is easier to quietly move along than to engage fully with the world around us.

When we actively work to observe what's here, we may find deep, dark wounds that have never seen the light of day. But miraculously, we also find deep, bright joy that our hearts have never known, at least not since the tragic loss that seemed to break us. If we allow one, we allow the other. When we experience the impact of feeling it all, we finally have an incentive to cultivate our courage. By taking off the tinted lenses, we may find unopened treasures patiently waiting to be released, just as our grief is also longing for our discovery and attention.

Pain and joy exist together, like two sides of the same coin. We have to be willing to observe both if we want to observe either. I have had so many experiences of this dynamic play out in my day-to-day life. As I began to understand the "pain-joy" coin analogy, I fervently denied that I would have to feel it *all* if I wanted to feel any of it.

But I wanted to feel good, without hurting. I wanted to be open to new life and joy even though two of my children had died. I didn't want to think about the grief. I wanted to keep moving so nothing landed on or stuck to me. Perpetual motion is a hell of a drug and can even be pragmatic in certain circumstances.

But eventually all things come to an end. The relief we may have experienced as a result of distraction loses its superpower over time. As with an addictive substance, we need more and more distraction to "protect" ourselves. As our grief hovers above and below over months and years, it grows anxious. Keeping it down requires more distractions, darker glasses, and learning to dodge ever-expanding currents of fear. We don't just imagine we are tired. We are tired. We are depleted. It's a big job to pull off consistently wearing tinted lenses, yet so many of us do it for so long.

After years of debilitating grief and fewer and fewer avenues to tame it, I finally tried to open my heart to joy. I wanted to feel it. I knew I was a shell of my core self. I knew it was time to turn the lights on and look carefully. And so I did: I turned them on— again and again and again.

But something unexpected happened, which made it even harder to stay committed to clear seeing. I started noticing that during occasions when I actually let my guard down and allowed a little joyful light to shimmer into my heart, it was always accompanied by unbearable, paralyzing pain.

As I let myself smile or belly laugh in an effort to take off the tinted lenses, I found my pain hitchhiking in on my joy. Sometimes it happened in the same instant, while other times it ran over me days or weeks later. I concluded that the emotional beating was the "price" I had to pay for happiness.

It seemed pointless for me to reach for joy. Over time my experience of life was that enjoying a party or going to work or taking a vacation were things that were necessarily coupled with agony. I didn't want this to be true. But occasions like the following one in Tennessee kept plaguing me, and I couldn't ignore them.

In early 2007, I was at a conference in Nashville to connect with my new community of certified legal nurse consultants. I had rarely left Zach at home and quite possibly had never taken such a trip since Alexis and Emmanuel had died. I would be traveling completely on my own. It was liberating. I was in a completely unknown environment, full of strangers I had never met. We were jointly focused on our emerging profession. I participated in breakout groups, where I got to meet tons of dynamic women who were also building their businesses.

I wasn't the mother whose kids died, the mother who later became a pediatric nurse. I wasn't the mother of a special-needs, g-tube-dependent, eight-year-old son. I was a woman, a consultant, and a professional. I didn't realize it, but as I traveled to a novel place and met new people, my armor started to come off a bit.

I found myself feeling confident, interested, and comfortable in my own skin (all unfamiliar states at that time). I remember hitting the treadmill early every morning and really trying to manage my energy so that I didn't miss anything. I was excited and felt like this was the new life I was seeking. No talk of dead babies, genetic diseases, or grief. I was in flow, on point, and determined.

So far, so good. Weren't these good reasons to have gone to this conference? Wasn't this the answer to a prayer I'd prayed a million times—to be able to "feel better" and "move on" finally? It seemed to be so. I reached for this possibility with hope, inspiration, and enthusiasm. Maybe there was still life ahead of me? For the first time in a decade, I felt "okay."

On the final evening of the conference, we were instructed to get dinner on our own. We were staying at the Gaylord Resort, where there were many options. Although I had a few invites to join others, I was feeling so empowered and at peace that I opted for alone time. I was so grateful and present, and I wanted to bask in the moments of quiet before traveling back to my whirlwind of a demanding life.

I got myself a burger and set up in a location where lighted fountains were about to be turned on for a small show. I was sitting on the stairs; no one else was around. When the fountains shot up, the music started, and the lights changed color and danced around the drops of water, I felt full. For a split second, I let myself feel the joy and freedom of eating, watching something pretty, and just being. It was a peace I hadn't felt since I could remember.

Then like a shotgun firing point blank through my midsection, leaving a gaping hole in my gut, my moment of peace was decimated. A young toddler with curly, girly hair and a loud giggle ran into the fountains. She pranced with delight! Her small feet carried her laughing, innocent spirit into, out of, and around those dancing fountains. Her mother was close behind, half-heartedly attempting to stop her. She, too, was in the moment, enjoying her daughter and letting joy be there.

When the shot hit me, I gasped, and the tear floodgates flew open uncontrollably. As much grief as I have endured in my lifetime, there are few moments in my history when I have wept with such fervor, abandon, and lack of ability to stop it as I did that night at the Gaylord in Nashville.

I tried to stand up slowly and take casual steps so I could get to my room and hide until the storm passed. But one small step turned into a full gallop, like when I feel I am going to vomit and think I can subtly walk to the bathroom, only to realize suddenly that I must run. Before I knew it, I'd fled right out of there and all the way to my hotel room, straight to the bed I'd sleep in for one more night. I called my mother. I told her I could not breathe. I cried and cried and cried.

Just thinking about that experience makes my stomach turn. It would be years before I realized what was happening to me, why that girl, joyful in that moment in that particular place, ignited such despair, such sorrow. I was so angry. I felt cheated. I felt betrayed. At the time, my bitterness grew as I thought about the fact that I never "got" to be happy and that the one time I did, I was punished by a full-on attack from the grief gremlin. My self-talk went something like this:

> *I should've known better. Happiness is not for me; it is for other people. My heart will never recover. Two of my children are dead. My living son is soon to follow. I should quit now and stop thinking I can ever be happy. I shouldn't have come here. I shouldn't have thought I could do something new. I shouldn't have thought I could be normal. I will never be okay. Ever.*

I flew home the next day, dejected, punished, and certain that happiness, joy, and fun were not available to me. It didn't matter how hard I worked or how much courage I had. I had pulled myself up by the bootstraps so many damn times, and it was all useless. I returned to Zach and his needs and the care teams that needed management. I forgot about being happy. I wouldn't dare take that chance again.

At the time, I noted that I didn't understand what was happening to me. But I think I do now: when I took off some of my armor to experience joy, the grief showed up, too. Since I never made space for either, they were competing for air, jumping out with great intensity like passengers trying to board the last roller-coaster ride before the park closed.

It would take me years to fully absorb this concept. But like many other similar experiences, this was the beginning of realizing that observing is not a selective process. This is how I learned that if we get still, find our equanimity, and let it all be here, we will experience all of it. If I open my heart to joy, I open it to pain—and the other way around.

Alternatively, I can leave the tinted lenses on, the blinds closed, and the lights off. But if I do that, I will never be more than a hollow shell of a woman going through the motions, determining my self-worth and identity solely on the basis of the value I bring to the lives of others and not to my own.

Practical Application: Cultivating Fresh Eyes

Unlike the first two stepping stones, this one may feel a bit more concrete because we already have a general sense of what is meant by the word "observation." The new element here, and the one we are focused on practicing, is to look at the full 360-degree surround of our perception. We move from selective observation ("I can only tolerate seeing things that make me feel 'good' or 'safe'") to all-inclusive observation ("I trust myself enough to allow what is here to reveal itself").

Sense perception is an integral way to experience the world we are in. I have found it helpful to step into each one of my sense perceptions to get to know all of them. Eventually they begin to work in concert. Our eyes, ears, tastebuds, and smelling and feeling abilities collaborate to produce a richer experience of what is here.

The goal of getting really good at observation is to develop an intimate relationship with each of our individual five senses so that they can play well together and help us access a sixth, conjoined, and harmonious sense we can call instinct, intuition, a "knowing," calm abiding, presence, and feeling of "being in the moment."

For each of the five senses below, you will find two practical applications. All the applications should be practiced in the absence of external stimulation when possible. In other words, if you are focused on "sight," make sure you are not cluttering up your inputs with music in the background or the loud sound of construction work. Focus on one sense perception at a time to see if you can gain a new understanding of what it means to truly observe and get to know something intimately.

Our ultimate goal with observation is to cultivate an integrated "sixth sense," the end result of aggregating all sensory input at a given moment. As we learn to layer in all forms of input, these layers begin to complement each other. I will discuss this in greater detail in the integration chapter in Part Three of *The Healing Path*.

1. *Sight*
    a. Adjust your TV volume setting to mute. Next time you are watching something, quiet the volume and look carefully at the images on your screen. How comforting or disturbing might those images be without narrative? Do they reflect content you want to place in your mind? Are you surprised by what you see?
    b. Bring home a flower that has not yet bloomed. Look at it closely on a daily basis. Watch it expand into its own unique beautiful identity. Notice the petals, colors, the shape of the stem in the water. See if in your observation of the flower, you can almost feel it trying to express itself a little more each day.

2. *Sound*
    a. Listen to a piece of music that does not have lyrics. Try to unpack the different sounds and instruments. Close your eyes and just listen. What do you hear?
    b. Try to notice a plane flying overhead, a lawn mower in the distance, the clock ticking, or the refrigerator humming in the background. You may discover a sound that was always there but that you never actually heard before now.

3. *Taste*
    a. Drink a full glass of water first thing in the morning. Before coffee and flavored beverages, just experience the miracle of plain, clean, fresh drinking water. Notice how it tastes.
    b. Eat your food without adding salt or sugar. If you normally add a little something extra, don't. Skip it this time. Try to actually taste what you are eating. Is it actually food you are consuming? Or is the food a vehicle for condiments and chemicals?

4. *Smell*
    a. If that flower that you purchased is blooming (from the sight application), close your eyes, then try to absorb and really notice the aroma. One of my favorite scents is that of a lily in bloom. It can be novel to use your sense of smell, absent other sensory input, to see which flowers have an aroma and which do not.

    b. Next time you are about to eat something fabulous, pause and close your eyes. Let the full manifestation of freshly baked bread, for example, wash over your sense of smell. See how it feels to enjoy something tasty through your sense of smell, instead of just taste and appearance.

5. *Touch*
    a. Put some gloves on. Close your eyes, then hold a neutral object in your hands, like keys or a hairbrush. See if you can get to know that object only through the sense of touch. What descriptors might you use to convey what is in your hand? Notice how challenging it is to describe something that you can't directly feel.
    b. Now take your gloves off, and hold that same object. What descriptors would now come to mind? Elements of smoothness, temperature, and size may come into play. Observe the stark difference in your ability to actually feel what you are touching now that the gloves are not a barrier.

These are just a few of the endless observation techniques we can try. Remember, we are not trying to just "see" an object, smell it, or feel it as much as we are trying to know a thing intimately by applying the skill of observation. So often we miss the depths of an experience because when we brace against everything, we limit our perception and keep a narrow viewpoint.

This can happen when we are grieving. We only see things through a limited, painful window; that's to be expected for a period of time. But when our fractured viewpoint born of pain becomes a way of life, we begin to miss more than our deceased loved one. We can miss life in its entirety. Paying attention during the process of observation helps us become more receptive, so more and more of what is meant by "life" will be able to reveal itself. If we aren't paying attention, we have no idea what we are missing even though it has been here and will always be here whether or not we observe and take notice.

Learning to exercise the skill of "real seeing" is the transformation we are going for. Sense perception is a material way to strengthen our observation skills. Trying some of these action steps may open your awareness to all that you could be missing by only allowing certain things into your experience.

As the Tony Award-winning musical *Hamilton* suggests, we must "Look around! Look around!" We must take it all in—that is, if we want to heal.

Six

Closing Thoughts

And this is presence: stillness, equanimity, observation.

These are the foundational pavers we can lay to build our own healing paths. Without them, we meander through an unmarked terrain. We don't feel much. We don't create much. We can "do" plenty. But our deeds are dry and passionless: they are expressions of forced energy that have no momentum of their own. FIDO (remember, Fuck It, Drive On) is the prevailing philosophy. One foot in front of the other becomes survival. Yes, we escape pain, but we give up so much more that we don't even know exists.

There is no magic remedy when it comes to easing the pain of grief. But what has been true for me is that resisting it is futile. There is no "getting over" my losses. There is only getting straight into them. By integrating my painful experiences with the joyful ones, I can show up as myself.

Bracing against the pain just delays it. When we hide from our grief, we need to create great distractions from the inevitable forks in the road. These are the choice points that repeatedly provide us with new opportunities to decide whether we will allow all of who we are to be here, including our scars, or hide and do anything we can to stay unconscious.

Getting still can be an intimidating and certainly uncomfortable experience, but it can be done in small doses. Only when we allow ourselves to settle and to process what is actually here do we even know what we are dealing with. When we take away the comfort measures (which don't work anyway) and defense mechanisms, we say yes to what's real, even if for the first time in our lives.

As we learn to tap into equanimity, we may find relief in the acceptance that everything is allowed to be here. We begin to exhale as we are washed over by the idea that it is okay for us to be here, too, and so are *all* of the many aspects of our unique experience.

Honing the skill of observation allows us to see what is here as the dust of our grief settles from time to time. Clear seeing is a practice of routinely abandoning our long-held associations, prejudices, and beliefs about all things and taking a fresh look around. Repeat often.

Since the word "heal" is part of the word "health," we cannot be whole and healthy without being on a path of healing. This approach is a guiding philosophy more so than a goal to be achieved. But we won't ever be released from the work it takes to get still, embrace everything as it is, and see what is actually here. When our hearts are broken, there is no getting around the fact that healing is *work*. And it is exhausting.

But it is also hard work to deny, hide, fake, pretend, mask, and anesthetize. When we stop using our energy to cover our scars from ourselves and others and learn to wear them as medals of love, a new landscape emerges. Like arriving over the peak of a mountaintop after a long journey up, we discover a whole other way of living that we didn't know was possible.

My hike up the mountain resulted in the end of my twenty-five-year marriage, leaving my dream home, and submitting my resignation from an established corporate career. But the view up here is stunning, the air is crisp and cool, and the landscape is a complete surprise. I am now afforded the opportunity to live with a freedom I have never felt before. It's the liberation that comes from intentionally engaging in the ongoing process of healing and therefore living.

An important element of my healing path now is to expand my connection with others in order to provide support and encouragement. Once you start paving your own healing path and doing the work it takes to stay on it, you will learn to wear your scars as medals, too. By practicing compassionate presence, we can normalize this courageous and authentic style of living and transcend the grief that has kept our hearts compartmentalized and isolated for far too long.

The first three stepping stones of this path are not to be taken lightly. When adequately implemented, they are game changers. The aggregate outcome of learning to sit still, allow, and observe is that we find ourselves to be *part of life instead of constantly bracing against it*. Instead of looking for shelter constantly, we cultivate the courage to allow the "being" part of human being to take shape. There is nothing to do. There is nothing to fix. There is just now.

Years ago, I watched an episode of *Dr. Phil*; he was talking about the role that physical intimacy plays in our marriages and/or adult relationships. According to Dr. Phil, when we are having regular sex with our partner, it constitutes about 10 percent of the relationship. But when we are not, it takes up more like 90 percent.

I see grief in a similar manner. When we are paying attention to it, allowing it, nurturing it, and caring for it, even if that means calling in sick from time to time, eating a box of chocolate-covered pretzels, and binging out on a Netflix series, it can take up a small percentage of our energy and our lives. But when we resist it and don't let it have a place at the table or anywhere else, the grief morphs into demanding most, if not all, of our energy.

I am not suggesting that sex and grief are the same or that this is a direct correlation of percentages. Rather, I am saying that the idea of "healing" or "feeling better" as an end game, a destination or a goal to be "achieved," is not the way I have personally experienced healing. I have learned the hard way that if I don't handle my grief, my grief handles me. For the most part, handling it just means letting it be here and not banishing it to the dark woods when I am in my warm house with a sign saying "Keep Out!"

Grief is a part of us that is here to stay, whether we want it or not. When we honor it, allow it, and are gentle with it and don't minimize its presence, the energy it takes from us decreases. But when we ignore it, run from it, and expect or desire it to be gone and when we stay numb, it can take over our lives, depleting the energy of every cell in our bodies.

Grief is different for everyone. There is no path to healing, except the one we create for ourselves. The path I initially built to carry out the FIDO tradition robbed me of the necessary processing of grief that was swirling inside me like a ravenous cancer.

From what others could see on the outside, I was bringing home the bacon, frying it up in a pan, and making certain my feeding-tube-dependent, tiny young man had every type of support known to humankind.

On the inside, my pain waited in the shadows. Every time I felt sad and didn't let myself ask questions or show compassion for my experience, it took a little more of me to fight it. Every time I lost a patient at work and made it my business to support the shocked, bereaved parents because "I knew how it felt" instead of getting the hell out of there, I cut off pieces of myself that I hated to look at. I gave them no time, no energy, no oxygen.

Sure, every once in a while, I would lose my shit. I would drink too much, feel sorry for myself, and fall apart here and there. But in those scenarios, my grief was in charge of my life instead of being part of it. With unattended pain calling my emotional shots, my reactions were irrational. They looked something like wanting to drive off the highway instead of going to work or excusing myself from a work dinner to weep in the bathroom stall because some group discussion about family (especially people's kids was hitting too close for me to conceal my visceral, acute panic.

As I grew into middle age, grief became unavoidable. I was just too tired to keep fighting. Grief was taking 90 percent of me, and the rest of the world, myself included, had to fight for the remaining 10 percent that wasn't unconsciously already spoken for.

Healing is the ongoing relationship we have with our scars. For me, giving up the fight to hide my scars from the world and to start honoring them as medals of love has paved the way for a healing path to emerge. I realized I was the one who was actively choosing to live a "dis-integrated" life, with different versions of myself blocking a major part of who I am. I now understood that I could choose differently.

It took a whole lot of practice to change, especially since I was so skilled at hiding and resisting being a whole person. And it is a practice, not somewhere to get as in an end game. The practice of change looks something like pausing when I feel something that makes my heart race. Or journaling when I am confused or overwhelmed so that I can name and connect with what's happening.

Changing for me also meant turning toward my pain with a welcoming grace and respect. Instead of seeing my pain as my flaw or weakness, I began to recognize that it is actually my greatest strength. Because I am still here.

As a friend who is also a loss survivor often poignantly says with her adorable Southern drawl, *I've survived 100 percent of my worst days, and this one won't do me in.* That is something to be proud of, not something to minimize or deny.

Little adjustments in how I see my grief and how I respond to its presence have helped me spiral up into becoming a whole and mostly fully integrated person, instead of dialing it in to fit the situation. The healing path is about making these small changes, day by day, and using these practices to pave the way for a different experience of life to emerge. The healing path is not about getting anywhere. It's about feeling safe where we are. It's about saying yes to our whole selves by taking courageous steps in the direction of self-compassion, love, and acceptance.

It's about a personal knowing, that we can handle whatever is happening even if it threatens to destroy us. We may not like it. But we are capable. We feel adequate. And that is the difference between running from ourselves and being ourselves.

Spoiler alert: We can't accomplish our dreams or goals if we are stagnant in survival mode anyway. Fear does not breed creative solutions to complex challenges. These first three stepping stones are about letting go of fear so we can make room for actual creation to evolve.

Afterword

The next volume of this three-part book series—*The Healing Path, Part Two: Stay Grateful*—will take you into the second phase of constructing the healing path. Sharing my personal experiences of grief will shift from the lens of a grieving young mother to that of someone surviving the heartbreaking experience of losing a loved one to death by suicide.

In *The Healing Path, Part Two: Stay Grateful*, I introduce and explore three additional steppingstones to expand your newfound ability to stay present. These next steps are gratitude, identity, and creation, all of which provide fuel for our healing. Learning to play with all three together will comprise the next phase of healing path construction.

In the meantime, do not suffer in silence. Loneliness emerges for all of us when we are grieving: it is one of the hardest effects of losing a loved one. It is also the fast ramp to chronic conditions like anxiety and depression. The fastest way to intervene on our own behalf when loneliness begins to brew is to *connect*. Connect with life.

Hug someone who loves you and won't let you go. Look in the mirror up close, and notice the life force behind those curious eyes, which are beaming and moving constantly. Walk in nature to be reminded that we are each a source of creation, as much as we are the result of it. Pet your dog. Watch a sunrise. Drink cool, clean water if it is available. Put down the smart device. Turn off social media and news for as long as possible. Instead of noise, flood your brainwaves with a calming piece of music, an inspirational experience you read about, or anything that can pull you from the depths of aloneness and into oneness with all of life's energy.

Don't wait until you are paralyzed with pain, fear, and anxiety before breaking ground for your healing path. We can and will learn together to create steppingstones that help us clear a path. *The Healing Path, Part Two: Stay Grateful* is about learning to embody the spirit of gratitude in a way that allows inner transformation to unfold, not in spite of profound loss but because of it. Once you have begun weaving stillness, equanimity, and observation into your life, your healing path is taking shape, and you are ready to move onto the next phase of building this path—staying grateful.

Made in United States
Orlando, FL
16 September 2024